EVERYDAY ETHICS

EVERYDAY ETHICS

The daily decisions you make & how they shape the world

DR SIMON LONGSTAFF

*This book is dedicated to Suzie Longstaff —
my partner in life — a woman of keen
intelligence, profound good sense
and boundless decency.*

First published in 2017
by Ventura Press
PO Box 780, Edgecliff NSW 2027 AUSTRALIA
www.venturapress.com.au

10 9 8 7 6 5 4 3 2

National Library of Australia cataloguing-in-publication data:
Author: Longstaff, Simon
Title: Everyday Ethics
ISBN 978-1-925183-42-9 (Print)
ISBN 978-1-925183-55-9 (Epub)

Design and typesetting by Alissa Dinallo
Cover and internal illustrations by Alissa Dinallo

CONTENTS

PREFACE

Picture these situations:

- Sitting in a room in Thailand, I am surrounded by senior military officers, most of them generals, from twenty-five nations in the Asia–Pacific region. One of them, to my right, has just said, 'The truth is that we torture people.' People do not shout out in outrage: they connect, seeking to understand how such a circumstance might be possible.

- In Brazil, I am standing at the site of a calamity—a failed tailings dam that has caused people to die, displaced communities, disrupted the regional and national economies, and wrought deep environmental damage. I am not there to judge; I am there to help those responsible form a view about how to do what is ethically right, as opposed to legally required.

- I am with a family whose father's health has failed. He is fed through a tube, and for some he seems to exist rather than live. A number of family members want to take every medical opportunity to preserve his life; others would like to scale back the medical intervention so that their father's inevitable movement towards death is not impeded.

- A gay man has been bullied to a point where his life has become unbearable. He sits before me sobbing. All his hopes for a better life have been dashed on the rocks of another man's carelessness.

✗ A cabinet minister, riven by anguish, needs someone to talk to about a career-defining—indeed, life-defining—moment of truth. It is vital that nobody knows the conversation took place. There is no need to provide a 'solution': what is needed is simply a safe place to work through the options without fear of being compromised.

These are scenes from my life. They are not the most dramatic, and they are not necessarily those of greatest consequence. Nor are they, perhaps, what you might expect if someone were to ask, 'What does a philosopher actually do?'

Of course, not all philosophers work in the way I do. Most of those who are earning a salary work in academic institutions. They research, write and teach, but usually with other academics as their focus. A few, such as the great, if occasionally mistaken, Peter Singer, change the world, their ideas—and, in Singer's case, the authenticity of his life—inspiring new understanding that shapes the day-to-day choices of ordinary people and not just academic discourse. Indeed, there are more philosophers of this kind than you might think. Philosophy is the great wellspring of knowledge: science, economics, politics, art, you name it, they are all either a direct offshoot of philosophy or are shaped by its disciplines.

For all that, though, it is rare to find philosophers out on the street, their sleeves rolled up, ready to embrace the nitty-gritty of life. So, how and why did I find myself doing exactly that, every second Tuesday at lunchtime in Sydney's Martin Place?

My initial exposure to philosophy came through the classical texts— in particular, the works of Plato, through which we come to know Socrates. I first encountered Socrates when reading of his last days, his trial and condemnation by male citizen jurors chosen by lot. Like those who accused and judged him, Socrates was a citizen of democratic Athens, at that time the leading city-state in the ancient world. Socrates taunted his judges, as if willing them to impose the penalty of death. They obliged. He then insisted that the execution proceed. Plato paints a picture of serene death, brought on by the poison hemlock. The reality was probably far more disturbing.

Having learnt about Socrates' death, I wanted to know more about his life. What had he done to cause such offence? Where had he done these things? And why?

One of the aspects of Socrates' life that attracted my attention was his desire to work in public places — most often in the marketplace, or *agora*, of Athens — along with the fact that he combined his role as a philosopher with that of a citizen. For him, doing philosophy was a part of being a citizen.

I was only sixteen when I left school. Lacking money to go to university and having exhausted my share of the family's limited resources, just three days after my seventeenth birthday I started work as a 'service attendant' (a euphemism for cleaner) at a BHP-owned manganese mine on Groote Eylandt, just east of Arnhem Land in the Northern Territory.

Being there — being cared for by the Aboriginal people of Anindi-lyakwa and, no less, the miners of Alyangula and Ndunga — changed me irrevocably. It also fired my interest in the world and how we make sense of it. Perhaps other experiences in my life had already opened me up to larger questions. The death of my mother, when I was seven, was undoubtedly the most momentous of those, but in its wake many other events (good and ill) have made it impossible not to dwell on some of life's larger questions.

But it was the grounding I received on Groote Eylandt that made me imagine Socrates in the marketplace as something of a 'kindred spirit'—albeit one with a genius, character and commitment that would dwarf anything I might hope to exhibit.

After Groote Eylandt, my life was anything but predictable. I studied some law, then graduated with a degree in education and taught in schools. I fell in and out of love and back in again. I married. And I was accepted into Magdalen College, Cambridge, where my progression from cleaner to philosopher was completed—not such a big leap as one might imagine.

Eventually, the role at The Ethics Centre (known as the St James Ethics Centre for its first twenty-five years) became available. The great attraction was that this role was as part of a 'start-up', affording me the opportunity to create something whereby I might be able to pursue my Socratic ideal of the philosopher as citizen. There was, however, a complication. The founder of The Centre, St James' Anglican Church in King Street, Sydney, and supporters from business and professional circles had envisaged a not-for-profit organisation. Indeed, when I started at The Centre there was only enough money to pay my salary for nine months. That was it. We would have to earn the funds needed or devise ways of attracting donations, or both.

This was not a great state of affairs, and a quarter of a century later the situation remains the same—no capital and an annual scramble to keep The Centre's doors open. The redeeming feature, though, is that the will to survive concentrates your attention on the people you hope to serve: you cannot sit atop the mountain and dispense wisdom; instead, you need to be mindful of real needs and serve present interests whenever and wherever the opportunity arises, and while doing this you need to uphold the integrity of your defining purpose, values and principles.

The Ethics Centre has survived a number of its own 'near-death experiences' caused by a lack of funding. It has been sustained by the goodwill and generosity of many people and by pursuing a remarkably varied range of opportunities.

Although driven by necessity, a diverse portfolio of activities has conferred one considerable benefit. It has allowed The Ethics Centre to recognise and apply a series of ethical 'patterns' that would not have been evident if we had focused on a single area. Applying these patterns to new areas of engagement has, in turn, generated considerable value for those with whom we have worked over the years.

Although there is something of the 'accidental' in the forces that have thus far shaped my work, I believe that opportunity and intent have coincided. For me, it is sad (if understandable) that relatively few philosophers choose to walk in Socrates' footsteps. Philosophical debate can be ferociously difficult and technical in its precision; arcane terminology is sometimes needed if progress is to be made. Yet the best philosophers are able to translate even the most difficult passages into the language of the ordinary person. I am not the most gifted of original thinkers. Realising this, I have done what I can to make philosophy—and especially my area of focus, ethics—more accessible.

Which brings me to this book. It is not a work of scholarship. I have done that kind of work before, for a different readership, in a different context. No, this book is for the bulk of my fellow citizens, not the experts. My purpose is to promote involvement and greater understanding. Although my opinions will become clear enough, I do not aim to preach or cajole. Rather, I invite you to test and challenge my opinions and the reasons on which they are based.

The range of topics discussed here is broad. Not vast; just broad. I sought others' advice about what they think is of interest or importance in everyday life. No doubt I missed some obvious candidates; no doubt I will be told this. Fortunately, a book of this kind can have a life online, with sections expanded over time to fill the gaps.

Most of the topics dealt with pose serious questions. A number of them are of such weight as to deserve an entire book of their own. Instead, I have opted to be as brief as possible, 'cutting to the chase', as they say. My aim is not to settle matters: it is to provoke reflection and discussion. I do not offer a handbook for 'good' living: rather, I offer the bare outlines of a map for navigating the landscape. Everyone has to make their own journey, finding their way from within the cockpit of their own lives.

It is quite possible that I express views here that do not necessarily support views I have expressed in other places and at other times. That is as it should be: we all change, and these are my current thoughts. I stress that they are of this time and are open to revision in the light of better argument, new evidence, and so on. Like Socrates, I am comfortable with not 'knowing'.

The philosopher is not some kind of special breed. Every person can be a seeker of wisdom. None of us is bound to be just one thing or another. Being human is both a wonderful and a formidable challenge. We can set some elements of that challenge aside or we can choose to embrace them.

If you are inclined to read on, please do so as a fellow traveller. Be open to the possibility that philosophy in general—and ethics in particular— need not be just part of what you do: it can be an aspect of who you are.

AN INTRODUCTION TO ETHICS

Every day of our lives is punctuated by points of decision. Some of the decisions will be momentous, remembered for decades; most will go unnoticed, by us and by others. Yet all our choices matter: taken as a whole, they shape our lives and contribute to the rhythms of the world.

Philosophers from all cultural landscapes have spent millennia thinking about the nature of these choices and how they might be directed towards living a 'good' life. In the West, discussion about these matters is called ethics. It begins with a simple, practical question that ancient Greek philosopher Plato ascribes to his friend and teacher Socrates: 'What ought one do?'

The two most important things about this question are its practical focus and its broad application to day-to-day living. The practical focus comes from a recognition that life demands an immediate response to most questions. If children are trapped inside a burning house, there is no time to be wasted in speculation. You need to make an immediate decision about how to respond. And if the answer is that you must try to rescue the children, you are obliged to act, to attempt the rescue.

But ethics is not just about what you should do in extreme cases of that kind. It is also about the ordinary questions of daily life. Do I buy eggs laid by free-range chooks or the cheaper ones from caged birds? Do I tell my best friend I saw her boyfriend kissing another girl? Do I lie to my grandmother by telling her I will wear the jumper she has knitted for me, even though it's the ugliest jumper in the world? Although questions to do with the death penalty, same-sex marriage and euthanasia are correctly labelled 'ethical' questions, this should not blind us to the fact that ethics touches virtually every decision we make.

Indeed, if you look around at the world we live in, the scope and importance of ethics soon become obvious. The first thing you realise is that nearly everything we encounter could have been different. For example, the ancient Egyptians could have built colossal, awe-inspiring stone cubes. The fact that the world has pyramids is a consequence of choice. The same is true of other things, both monumental and minor in scale: our buildings, our technology, our fashions—all these could be different from what we find. It is a matter of choice.

Unfortunately, not every human choice gives rise to something beautiful, useful or benign. Choice has also brought death camps, nuclear weapons, factory farming, global warming, and all that degrades us and the planet we share.

There is, however, a way to understand the basic structure of human choice, which can be described as a universal grammar, as social DNA, as an architecture for choice. These analogies work to a degree; they help to explain what is going on below the surface, so that we can understand and perhaps better control what shapes our decisions and therefore makes the world as it is, including the little parts of it we control through our everyday actions.

THE STRUCTURE OF HUMAN CHOICE

The field of ethics begins with a simple practical question about what any one of us ought to do in particular situations and during the course of our life. Many differing answers to this question have been offered over time. Some are grounded in religious belief; others in secular thought. Later in this section we look at some of the main approaches developed over the centuries, but for now I want to set out the basic structure of ethics, which can be viewed through the prism of values, principles and purpose.

VALUES

VALUES   PURPOSE   PRINCIPLES

Any person making an unconstrained choice always chooses the option they believe to be good or best. Imagine a simple choice—say, between eating an apple or an orange. Further, imagine that you can choose freely. No one will force your hand, either literally or metaphorically. If you choose the apple this is because for you, at that time, it is a good or better choice. Another person might choose the orange. For that person, at that time, it will be a good or better choice.

Now, we might not know why another person makes their choice. They might prefer the colour orange, or they might think it the healthier option, or the taste of an orange might trigger a fond memory. Instead, the one thing we know for certain is that they think that, in all the circumstances, the orange is good and, indeed, better than the apple.

This seems obvious: people don't freely choose the bad or worst option. We might not agree with their choice—maybe even thinking it foolish or dangerous—but for the person doing the choosing it is good.

This axiom—'If you allow a person an unconstrained choice they will always choose the option they think is good or best'—gives rise to the first element in the basic structure of ethics. The reason for this is that it leads to an obvious second question: 'If people with a free choice are always going to choose what is "good", then what is or should count as "good"?'

There are plenty of possible answers to this. Some people might answer by listing qualities such as liberty, justice, love and harmony; others might list success, fame, power and prestige. Whatever the list might include, those things are classed as 'values'.

Values are like 'guideposts', giving you direction on your life journey. Once established, they give direction to any choice that involves the 'goods' they define.

So, if someone tells you they have a particular set of values, you are entitled to believe that, if one of those values is at stake when a choice needs to be made, the person will choose the option that gives them what they have told you is good. For example, a person who says they value 'trust' can reasonably be expected to choose options that express or build trust. If instead they pick an option that involves deception, it is reasonable to assume that they don't understand the concept of 'trust' or are insincere or cannot link what they say and do to any practical degree.

The list of values humans perceive as good is vast. Some people worry that the list is so long as to make the varying lives of individuals, communities and cultures incomprehensible. But things are actually less complicated than that.

The first thing to be aware of is some basic facts about the human condition — that we are born, that we die, that we live under the same sky, and so on. The elements common to the human experience tend to encourage a degree of convergence in what we think is good and therefore in our values. Some of this arises from the requirement to meet basic human needs. We all need food, shelter and a minimal level of personal safety and security, so it shouldn't surprise us that these things are considered good the world over. These common goods extend beyond material necessity; for example, people value friendship, compassion and the many other building blocks of community.

The second thing to be mindful of, though, is that shared values can be expressed in differing types of behaviour in different settings. Some groups of people might express friendship by sharing a meal together; others might express it by spending time together engaging in common leisure activities; yet others might see gift giving or other forms of ritual behaviour as conferring membership of a friendship group.

As a consequence, it is important not to judge relative strangers negatively just because they engage in unfamiliar forms of behaviour. I have seen, for example, Australian business people react suspiciously when offered a gift in a country such as Japan. Such gifts are often offered by the Japanese as an expression of friendship. Unfortunately, it is not uncommon for strangers to misinterpret the offer — potentially causing offence to their Japanese host. The point is this: both value 'friendship' as something good, but they express the value differently and in accordance with their particular culture. Once it is understood that the gift is a token of esteem (and not an attempt to secure an improper advantage), all is fine. Many difficulties could be avoided if we were more sensitive to the fact that shared values can be expressed differently in cultural settings other than our own.

There is another aspect to otherwise shared values that gives rise to genuine differences — not just in behaviour but in connection with the choices we make as individuals and societies. Communities have many values in common, but the relative priority of those values can vary considerably. If, for example, you had conducted a survey of US citizens on 10 September 2001, asking them to list their values and rank them in order of priority, you would almost certainly have found 'liberty' nominated at or near the top of the list. The United States is a country where people can find the burning of their national flag deeply offensive, but in the name of liberty they will defend your right to burn it.

In contrast, if you had conducted the same survey on the same day in, say, China, the value of 'liberty' would have been nominated but not at or near the top of the list. Prime position would have been reserved for 'harmony', or a 'proper ordering of things'. The Chinese do, of course, recognise the value of liberty—just not at the expense of order in society. For that reason one could not get away with burning the Chinese flag as a form of political protest. It would not only be a serious insult; it would express (and potentially cause) disorder (loss of social harmony). 'Harmony' is not just valued by the government of China; it is a core value held widely among the Chinese people.

Of course, governments—here notionally the US and Chinese governments—appeal to, and sometimes exploit, the relative priority of values for their own political purposes. But when Americans appeal to 'liberty' and the Chinese to 'harmony' they are tapping into something almost palpable within the ethical landscape of their citizens.

The difference between what lies at the top of each list of values goes a long way to explaining the differing nature of each society. It is important to remember, though, that these differences might not be lasting: the relative priority of values can change from time to time.

I hypothesised that our survey was conducted on 10 September 2001, the day before terrorist attacks on the World Trade Center towers in New York and the Pentagon in Washington DC. Imagine now that the survey had been conducted in the United States just twenty-four hours later. Would those surveyed have still assigned top place to the value of liberty? No. Liberty would have moved down the list and the value of security would have taken priority. And that adjustment to the relative priority of Americans' values, rather than the events themselves, brought about dramatic and dangerous changes in the tide of history.

In the wake of the 9/11 attacks, the American people stopped reaching out their hand to take up the 'apple of liberty'; instead, they chose security, and in doing so have made some extraordinary changes. For example, in enacting the USA PATRIOT Act they have agreed to suspend one of the oldest of human liberties, *habeas corpus* (the right not to be held without charge, the right to be brought before a court). Additionally and all in the name of security, they have built new physical and technological barriers that control the flow of people. The dominant value of security has changed the face of the American nation—as it has in other countries, such as Australia.

All this has happened because of a change in the relative priority of the nation's values. I make no comment here on whether the change was justifiable; I simply note that it occurred and that the world has changed precisely as predicted in our axiom that if you allow a person an unconstrained choice they will always choose the option they think is good or best. At another time, in another place, the value of liberty might have been preserved relative to that of security: we might live more dangerous lives but with greater freedom. In that sense, after 9/11 the United States and the rest of the Western world became a little more like China, where liberty is 'sacrificed' for some other 'greater good'.

Discussion of global terror and national responses to its scourge might seem to draw us a long way from the discussion of everyday ethics, yet the role that values play in daily life is the same. Although we might not be conscious of how our values shape our choices, we follow those guideposts all the time. Indeed, there is no avoiding their effect.

At this point it is worth pausing to ask yourself several questions: What do you think is 'good'? What would you include in a list of values? How would you assign priority to the items in your list of values? And how would your values be expressed in practice?

PRINCIPLES

Many people assume that it is values alone that constitute the basic structure of ethics. Yet trying to live a good life by relying solely on values is like trying to run on one leg—something that is technically possible but is more likely to lead to a fall.

Suppose you have a friend who assigns top priority to the value of 'success'. One day they confide in you that they plan to achieve success in the sporting world by winning a gold medal at the coming Olympic Games. You know they have only modest sporting talent, so this comes as something of a surprise. But no, your friend says 'it's in the bag': they have found a foolproof strategy for cheating their way to the podium. You might well agree that it is 'good' to win a gold medal, but you would probably tell your friend their chosen path to success is not 'right'. Pressed to explain why you think this, you would most probably cite a principle to justify your position. It is principles that define for us what is 'right'.

Put simply, values are about what is good and principles are about what is right. If values are like guideposts helping you navigate the highways and byways of life, principles are their indispensable complement because, while values tell us where to head, principles tell us how to get there. That is, they regulate the means by which we secure the things we believe to be good.

For example, we might agree that it is good to go from Alice Springs to Melbourne, so the decision is made to head south. But how are we to proceed? By car? Will we make our way according to the speed limit, or will we go as fast as we can and hope to avoid detection? Will we drive on without a break, or will we stop from time to time to rest? Will we stick to the main road, or will we take a tourist route? It is principles that help us answer the 'how' questions once we have answered the 'where' question.

Confusion often arises about the difference between values and principles, and the words are often used interchangeably, without much consequence. If we are to understand the basic structure of human choice, though, we need to understand the particular character of principles.

The best way to explain the difference is to distinguish between 'thick' and 'thin' content. Values have thick content in that their central meaning is independent of the particular circumstances in which people find themselves. For example, the value of 'friendship' can be expressed in different ways in different cultures, but the central idea—that of affection, affinity, and reciprocal obligation beyond family—is held in common. On the other hand, despite their considerable power to affect conduct, principles have only 'thin' content. This becomes clear if we look at three classic principles:

THE GOLDEN RULE

Do unto others as you would have them do unto you.

THE SUNLIGHT TEST

We should do only those things we would be proud to be seen doing by those whose opinions we respect.

CONSCIENCE

We should act only according to a well-informed (and well-formed) conscience.

Each of these principles has its own history, and each provides a different basis for making practical decisions about how to secure the things we deem to be good. What they have in common, however, is that they do not provide any detailed information about how we should treat people, what we should be proud to do, or what a particular conscience might decide in a particular situation.

When it comes to principles, the thin content leaves a large amount of room for us to make decisions. Thus, one person's view of how they would like to be treated might differ from another person's: a member of a criminal syndicate might value only the esteem of other criminals; one doctor might in good conscience perform an abortion, whereas another might not.

In view of this, one might be inclined to question the point of principles: if their content is so thin, why bother with them at all? But we should not be fooled by the amount of freedom principles typically confer. Thin they might be, yet they are also powerful, and once they are adopted there is no hiding from them. If you claim for yourself the golden rule (Do unto others …) there is no escaping the conclusion that you do wrong if you treat someone in a way you would not like to be treated.

There are many other principles a person might adopt, and it is possible to uphold many at the same time as long as they are not mutually contradictory. For example, you could replace the golden rule, the sunlight test and conscience with alternative principles:

× the iron rule—Do unto others before they do it to you.

× the shadow test—Don't get caught.

× convenience—Do whatever feels good at the time.

A person who upheld these principles would make choices that are radically different from those made by someone adopting the first trio of principles. It is for this reason that a complete guide to good conduct must include both values and principles. Only when both components are present can we hope to understand the basis for human choice.

Again, it is worth pausing to ask yourself several questions: Can you identify any principles that guide your conduct? Can you see how those principles might be connected to your values? Are you running life's race on both legs or lurching along on just one?

PURPOSE

If there are so many possible values and principles from which to choose, and if their possible permutations are so numerous, how is a person to decide on what is 'good' and 'right'?

As noted, it is quite probable that there are some central values and principles that any community will need to adopt if it is to flourish. In his book, *The Abolition of Man*, CS Lewis provides an appendix[1] that lists the many values and principles humans have

---

1 Lewis, CS (1943), *The Abolition of Man*, https://archive.org/stream/TheAbolition-OfMan_229/C.s.Lewis-TheAbolitionOfMan_djvu.txt.

adopted, apparently independently, across divisions of culture, time and place. For example, in citing the 'Law of Mercy', he lists the following:

> The poor and the sick should be regarded as lords of the atmosphere. (Hindu. Janet, i. 8)

> Whoso makes intercession for the weak, well pleasing is this to Samas. (Babylonian. ERE v. 445)

> Has he failed to set a prisoner free? (Babylonian. List of Sins. ERE v. 446)

> I have given bread to the hungry, water to the thirsty, clothes to the naked, a ferry boat to the boatless. (Ancient Egyptian. ERE v. 446)

> One should never strike a woman; not even with a flower. (Hindu. Janet, i. 8)

> There, Thor, you got disgrace, when you beat women. (Old Norse. Hdrbarthsljoth 38)

> In the Dalebura tribe a woman, a cripple from birth, was carried about by the tribes-people in turn until her death at the age of sixty-six ...'They never desert the sick. (Australian Aborigines. ERE v. 443)

> You will see them take care of, widows, orphans, and old men, never reproaching them. (Redskin. ERE v. 439)

Nature confesses that she has given to the human race the tenderest hearts, by giving us the power to weep. This is the best part of us. (Roman. Juvenal, xv. 131)

They said that he had been the mildest and gentlest of the kings of the world. (Anglo Saxon. Praise of the hero in Beowulf, 3180)

When thou cuttest down thine harvest ... and hast forgot a sheaf ... thou shalt not go again to fetch it: it shall be for the stranger, for the fatherless, and for the widow. (Ancient Jewish. Deuteronomy 24:19)

One might explain the existence of such common currents of thinking as the result of coincidence or perhaps as evidence of subtle forms of cultural transmission. Or, as suggested, it could be that common aspects of the human condition have produced a common response.

Yet even CS Lewis's fairly short compendium leaves a large number of options from which we might choose. One approach that can help here is to identify a defining purpose.

Organisations (including occupational groups) are created by humans to serve specific purposes, and it is relatively easy to identify central values and principles relating to those purposes. Accountants and journalists should care about truth, the military about peace, doctors and nurses about health and wellbeing. Similarly, telecommunications companies have been established as a means of enabling us to keep in contact with one another, even over vast distances. We might therefore expect something of this purpose to be reflected in the ethical framework of a telecommunications organisation—in, say, a principle such as 'building and maintaining networks'.

In the case of individuals, however, it is much harder to specify the overall purpose of a human life—even though that difficulty has not deterred people from trying to do so. Among the popular options for expressing the purpose of human life are flourishing, to serve god (or gods) and enlightenment. Other options are closer to the types of things organisations choose. Rather than taking life as a whole, another possibility is to link questions of purpose to role or function, breaking life into more digestible chunks. Thus, a person might focus on aspects of their life (as a child, a sibling, a parent or a grandparent, say), or we might think of ourselves in terms of function (as a baker, a butcher or brewer, say). In all such cases we might ask what values and principles would be necessary for us to become the best we can be in the chosen role. What would be required to be a good baker, butcher, child or grandparent?

It would probably make life simpler if there were agreed lists of the central values and principles one should ideally uphold for each role or function we might perform during our life, but I am not aware of such things. Nevertheless, the idea of purpose can be a useful lens through which to look at what core values and principles might be adopted. Indeed, just thinking about one's purpose in life can itself be illuminating.

IN SUMMARY

Thus far, we have identified four elements that form the basic structure of human choice:

× the central question—What ought one do?

× values—These emerge in answer to the question, 'What is good?'

× principles—These emerge in answer to the question, 'What is right?'

× purpose—This can help determine the specific selection of central values and principles that might populate an ethical framework.

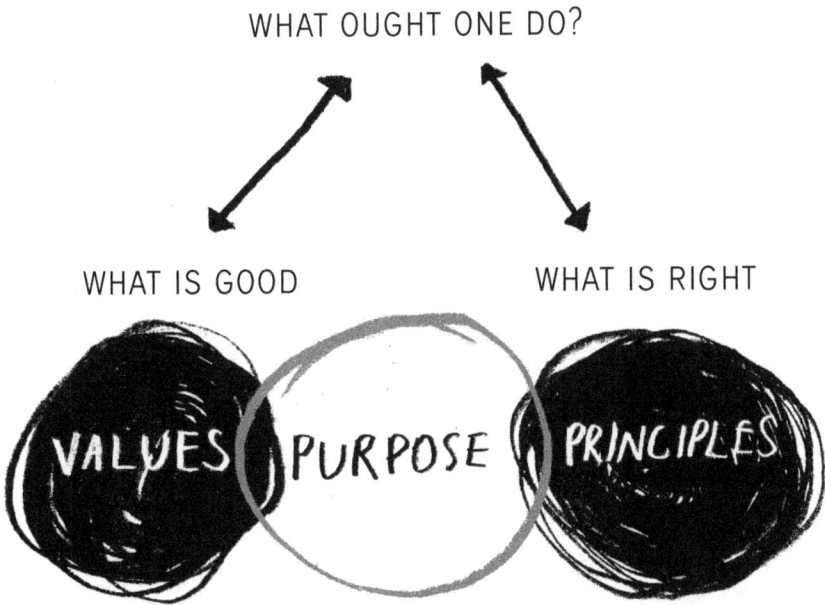

WHAT OUGHT ONE DO?

WHAT IS GOOD

WHAT IS RIGHT

VALUES PURPOSE PRINCIPLES

Fig. 1: The basic structure of human choice

This basic structure is applicable to all human societies at all times. It provides a universal grammar for understanding the structure of human choice, and if one can discern what an individual or group claims to be good and right (that is, their values and principles) it is possible to make sense of the choices they make.

Of equal importance is the notion that if you are able to shape the content of each of the boxes illustrated—values, purpose and principles—then you ultimately shape the choices people will make and in so doing shape the world as influenced by humans. This is one reason why people often compete for control of ethical systems. One can compel people to do one's will through the application of force or fear, but far more can be achieved by harnessing the efforts of willing allies making free choices within a common ethical system.

THE CONTEXT OF HUMAN CHOICE

The structure of human choice, as outlined, needs not only specific content if it is to come alive: it also needs to be understood and applied within a particular context. The primary aspect of this context is relationships—especially in terms of who is recognised as being worthy of ethical consideration. There are some people, known as 'ethical egoists', who attach significance to no one but themselves. There are, however, many more who look a little further afield, applying tight boundaries when considering who matters and who does not. For example, they might count members of their immediate family and close friends as worthy of consideration, but relative strangers might be considered 'fair game'.

One way to think of this is to imagine you have an umbrella that you can choose to make as large or as small as you want. Who will you keep dry? Who will you allow to get wet? And what are the circumstances, if any, in which you might change your mind? What you are imagining is 'circles of belonging', or 'circles of concern', depicting the range of individuals you think belong in your ethical universe or about whom you might be concerned.

Ethical egoists deploy the smallest of umbrellas — just wide enough to keep themselves dry. In contrast, some cultures go very wide, to the point where, for example, individuals and groups include within their circles of concern all other human beings. For some this might be a religious duty in recognition that all humans are made 'in the image of their creator'; others might include all human beings in recognition of a shared state of being; many other reasons are possible, too. Some cultures extend their circle of concern even further: for example, adherents of the Jain religion attribute ethical significance to all life, even creatures such as ants and gnats. Finally, like many of the world's indigenous peoples, Australia's First Peoples find ethical significance in all that is, including things that others consider inanimate; as a result, an Indigenous Australian can have kinship ties with plants, animals, and the spirits in rocks and other natural formations.

We all need to decide how wide we draw our personal circle of concern and how and where we locate others who will be affected by the choices we make and what we say and do.

MORALITY

ITS ROLE

As we have seen, the basic structure of ethics is relatively simple – just think of three boxes respectively labelled 'values', 'principles' and 'purpose'. Each box then needs to be filled with specific content. The finished package is a 'morality'.

On a day-to-day basis, our decisions are a reflection of an underlying morality. Even our habits have a moral foundation, albeit one that is often unconscious or obscure. Because of this, the control of morality has always been of interest to those wishing to exercise power. Although it is possible to force people to do your will, it is far more efficient and effective if they do so willingly, guided by an underlying moral framework.

But where do these frameworks come from?

The creation of moralities can be understood as a historical process in which different individuals and groups have competed to develop the best possible answer to Socrates' question, 'What ought one do?'. At first there is a babble of voices discussing potential answers. Eventually, there emerges a series of coherent responses.

For example, a Jewish answer emerges. Next to this and to one side are the Muslims and the Christians. There are various Buddhist voices, plus Hindus, Daoists, Confucians, Shintoists, Zoroastrians and so on. Then there are the Epicureans, the Stoics, the Utilitarians, the Kantians and more. What each group has in common is that it offers a curated set of values and principles that we can just plug into our lives and then put on 'play'.

The religions offer something additional to that offered by the various philosophies. Their packages include facets such as 'revealed truths', beliefs about the relationship between humans and the divine and the retelling of exemplary lives. The heart of their offering is, however, a framework for how an individual can live, shaping day-to-day decision-making in the context of a set of defined relationships and with a sense of purpose thrown in. The philosophers might be less comprehensive in their offering, but the basic framework is the same.

Each package is a 'morality'; each is meant to provide a 'ready reckoner' for living a good life; and each is meant to be applied in practice.

ITS PROBLEMS

It would be comforting to think that the challenge posed by Socrates' question can be so easily met. If only we could just pick, or absorb, a morality and move on effortlessly. But this is not how the human condition expresses itself.

The first difficulty to be reckoned with is that no moral framework yet developed provides the kind of certainty people long for in order to live a safe, untroubled life. This is not a result of shortcomings on the part of theologians or philosophers: they have spent thousands of years trying to build fully coherent systems that can provide guidance on what is good and right.

The inconvenient truth is that no amount of time, effort or brilliance can create a system that produces moral certainty.

Let's look more closely at the problem. Suppose you could assign a numerical value to mark the strength with which you hold each central value. You might assign, say, ten units to the value you hold most strongly as good and minus ten to something you consider most strongly to be bad. In an ideal world all your central values would point in the same direction. For example, you might be a person who values most strongly truth (ten units) and compassion (ten units). One would hope that truth and compassion would lead you in the same direction.

Consider, however, what might happen if someone you love (your mother, perhaps) shows you a dress she has just bought and asks you what you think. Maybe you will be pleasantly surprised by her good taste. But maybe you will not: she might have made what you think is a terrible choice that has the potential to embarrass her. It might be that your mother is good at taking criticism if it is sincere. On the other hand, she might be more delicate, the kind of person the truth will hurt, no matter how good your intentions are. In this situation your values of truth and compassion could come into conflict: if you tell your mother what you really think, you will hurt her.

When something like this happens, it is impossible to come up with a perfectly good or right answer. The result will be a 'null' answer, with values of equal weight pulling you in opposing directions. More on this later, but suffice it to say here that no religion, philosopher or theoretician has come up with an answer to this conundrum.

Quandaries such as this have led some people to give up on ethics. After all, if a system of ethics cannot provide certainty in connection with apparently simple questions, why bother thinking about it at all?

In despair, quite a few people head for one of two exits. They can bail out into a form of hedonism that involves letting go of the big questions entirely, taking the view that we might as well distract ourselves with something pleasant and let someone else sort out the mess.

The other, more dangerous, exit leads to the camp of the fundamentalists. Whatever the form—religious, political, scientific—the fundamentalists' siren song is the same: come here, cast down the burden of your uncertainty, and we will decide for you; all you need to do is obey.

In their worst forms, both hedonism and fundamentalism degrade the human condition. But even their milder forms can be damaging to those who would live an ethical, rather than a merely moral, life. The key to understanding the difference lies in knowing that it is possible to live a perfectly acceptable moral life without much thought or engagement. We can opt for a pre-packaged morality and develop a series of virtuous behaviours—habitually kind, habitually courteous, habitually honest and generous—attracting the admiration of all. The trouble is we would still be living a lesser life, at least as compared with the type of life a human being might seek to live. At this point we need to return to Socrates and his claim that the unexamined life is not worth living.

SOCRATES' PRIMARY CLAIM

In 399 BCE, Socrates was charged with two offences: impiety and corrupting the youth of Athens. His conduct as a citizen had been exemplary—he had been a brave soldier and he lived a modest life—but a number of powerful people objected to his teaching. This is because he asked difficult questions and in doing so cast doubt on conventional wisdom in Athenian society. His questioning caused some prominent citizens to appear foolish because he exposed the fact that they did not really understand concepts such as justice, which they claimed they were administering in the courts and elsewhere.

If we are to believe Plato's account of Socrates' life, it seems clear enough that Socrates did not set out to make others look foolish. One of his most consistent claims was that whatever wisdom he did possess lay in his awareness that he did not know much at all. Indeed, it was this recognition of ignorance that caused the Pythos at the Oracle of Delphi to deem him the wisest of all men. By employing dialogue (*elenchus*) as his preferred tool for exploring the limits of his own knowledge, however, Socrates drew into his circle people who assumed they already knew most of what was required of a citizen who deserved the esteem of their peers.

Although Socrates might never have intended to expose the ignorance of others, that was the effect of his contact with them. To make things worse, he did not go about his business in private places where any loss of prestige on the part of others might be shielded from public view. Instead, he took to the streets, most famously the Athenian *agora*, or marketplace. The effect of this was that onlookers would often witness the discomfort of some of Athens' most famous citizens when they faced Socrates' combination of questions and logic.

Poet William Blake wrote, 'Wisdom is sold in the marketplace where no one comes to buy.'[2] And so it proved for Socrates: his wisdom was not only unpopular with the community's leaders; it was also considered dangerously subversive because it was so appealing to many young Athenians. The young people took pleasure in the spectacle of their elders being shown to have intellectual shortcomings and delighted in the iconoclastic implications of Socrates' thought—the fact that he encouraged them to critically examine all that seemed to have been settled by older

---

2 Blake, W (2010), *The Four Zoas*, https://en.wikisource.org/wiki/Vala,_or_The_Four_Zoas/Night_the_Second p.35.

generations, including the question of the nature of the gods and their relationship with humankind.

This was too much for those with power and influence in Athens, and Socrates was put on trial, the penalty for the offences with which he was charged being death. The evidence is that most people did not want Socrates to die: they just wanted him to leave Athens so they could get back to their lives without this gadfly stinging them daily with his questions. As a result, when he was found guilty of the two charges, he was offered the option of exile. He refused to go into exile, though, insisting that the law be followed to the letter. He had used his skills to argue his innocence to no avail. If justice, impartially applied, demanded his death, then that was the fate he must endure—as must the people of Athens if they were found to have broken the law.

It was at about this time when, on addressing the court, Socrates is recorded as having uttered that most profound of statements: 'The unexamined life is not worth living.'[3]

I have spent much of my life thinking about what Socrates might have meant by this. Some of what I think is clearly described in what Plato says about Socrates' approach to philosophy and life. But much of what I think is based on my own process of trying to 'fill in the gaps'. As a consequence, what follows cannot be said to be an account of Socrates' own thinking. Instead, it is inspired by his life and words, and my aim is to do justice to what he might have said had we had the chance to discuss this face to face in an *agora* of our own making.

---

3 Plato (2013), *Apology*, http://www.gutenberg.org/files/1656/1656-h/1656-h.htm (trans. Benjamin Jowett).

THE ETHICAL LIFE

To understand Socrates' primary claim we need to begin with a 'worldly' observation about the human condition. This observation has the same self-evident character as the axiom (about unconstrained choice) we encountered when beginning our journey toward answering the central question of ethics, 'What ought one do?'

The observation is that, in general, human beings have the capacity to transcend the demands of instinct and desire. That is, we are not *bound* to act according to instinct; we are not *bound* to satisfy our desires, no matter how strong they are. Instead, we have the ability to make conscious choices and to act in accordance with what we think is good and right.

Some people might see a number of potential objections to this claim. The most obvious of these would be that the capacity to make conscious decisions is an illusion—that free will (genuine choice) is a fiction. The main basis for this is the notion that a universe predicated on the operation of cause and effect is one in which what is yet to happen has already been determined by past events, interactions, and so on. Other people might object to the idea of free will by appeal to scientific evidence—the way synapses relating to choice seem to fire before we become aware of our choice—or to pre-scientific conceptions such as those of fate or god's will.

Much could be said in response to such objections, including that quantum mechanics reveals a universe far less determined than once thought, that recent discoveries in neuroscience throw into doubt some of the claims about the order of events surrounding the conscious perception of choice,[4] and that most religions are founded on the assumption that humans have free will and are thus accountable for their choices.

Arguing the case for (or against) the existence of free will would make for a book in itself. Instead of doing that, I want simply to observe that, however the arguments and evidence might ultimately fall, the common human experience is that our ability to make choices is real. Perhaps we are deceived in this, but if that is the case it is a deception that helps define the human condition. The ability to make conscious choices is an important aspect of what it means to be human.

What then is the status of people who lack the individual, personal capacity to make choices? I argue that to be human is to belong to a 'class of beings' endowed with this capacity.

It should be noted that, on this account, intrinsic dignity is possessed by all humanity as a result of their belonging to a particular 'class of being'. That is, intrinsic dignity is not a function of individual capacity. A newborn child or a person of defective reason enjoys the intrinsic dignity of personhood as a member of the human race. It is on this foundation that all other human rights rest, and it is this notion that is captured in the common phrase 'respect for persons'.

As things stand, we do not know if other creatures have an equal or approximate capacity to transcend instinct and desire in order to make conscious, ethical choices. I am sceptical about this, but I have to admit I do not know. For example, if I think of a lion hunting

---

4 See Ananthaswamy, A (2012), 'Brain might not stand in the way of free will', *New Scientist*, 6 August, https://www.newscientist.com/article/dn22144-brain-might-not-stand-in-the-way-of-free-will/.

an impala I doubt that it pauses to think to itself, 'I'm hungry, but what about the impala's offspring?' I think the lion hunts, kills and eats without being troubled by scruples.

But that is not what is at issue here. The key point is that we do know that the 'class of being' to which humans belong has that defining capacity. For example, I know that countless men and women stand firm in the face of truly frightening situations, when every instinct would be to flee, or resist the temptation to take something they deeply desire. In many cases they are not defending a loved one, and nor are they concerned about being observed or restrained; instead, they are selfless and courageous in defence of a promise or an ideal, or they exercise restraint simply because they believe that to satisfy their desire would be wrong.

As noted, the capacity to make conscious choices — or at the very least to experience this capacity as real — is part of what it means to be human. This is not to deny humanity's 'animal' nature: it is merely to observe that this part of our nature, which we share with all other animals, is not necessarily determinative of our choices and conduct.

Why humans alone should have this capacity to transcend instinct and desire is open to debate. Some people offer an explanation grounded in religion. For example, the Mosaic traditions of Judaism, Islam and Christianity conceive of humankind as made in the image of God. This does not imply a physical resemblance; rather, it is the moral image of God as a being endowed with freedom that is thought to be reflected in the human condition — with all the potential difficulties entailed in being both free and obedient. Other explanations of the human capacity for rational choice look to science; for example, socio-biologists invoke the mechanisms of evolution.

It would take yet another book to explore these things, and theologians, scientists and philosophers will continue to wrestle with them for years to come. It is, however, unnecessary to settle the debate here: as I said, I merely aim to begin with a series of 'worldly' observations that are in my view self-evident. The claim that human beings are not bound by instinct or desire meets the test. We might not know why this is so, but it is enough to recognise that it is obviously true of human beings in general.

The importance of this for understanding Socrates' statement that an unexamined life is not worth living is that in my opinion he was using a pithy observation to say something like the following:

× The best kind of life for a human being is a fully human life.

× A fully human life is one in which we transcend our animal nature and go beyond instinct and desire in order to make conscious decisions about how we are to live.

× This means we should think for ourselves; that we should live an 'examined life'. That is, the examined life is the fullest form of life for a human being. Anything less is not worth living—at least if you aspire to live a fully human life.

It is as though each of us lives in a house with many rooms— some easier to enter and more comfortably furnished than others. Every human house contains a room in which one might examine life. It might not be the most comfortable of rooms, and spending time in it will not necessarily make you safer, wealthier or more popular. Further, there is no compulsion to enter. It might be more convenient to remain outside, leaving the door closed. But, if this is what you do, can you ever claim to have *lived* in the house?

Earlier I discussed morality and the risk that a moral life might well be lived according to habit and convention, without any continuing process of conscious reflection. To live such a life is to live in only part of the human house. To live an ethical life, an examined life, requires that we walk into the room reserved for reflective practice. And, in doing so, we walk in the footsteps of Socrates.

We must be mindful, however, that the choice of such a life does not guarantee a reward. Socrates paid the price for being fully human: it would have been easier to blend in with the herd, to bare one's throat and submit to the most powerful. To live an examined life is to expose oneself to constant questioning and to resist the temptation to follow a life of unthinking custom and practice.

Such a life calls for courage, honesty, integrity and more. Indeed, it is possible to start with the idea of an examined life, as outlined, and build on this foundation an entire ethical framework—complete with a rich and detailed account of the values and principles that such a purpose entails.

But developing the details of that framework is a task for another time. For now, I am proposing that an ethical, or examined, life is the kind of life we should aim to live. Such a life is not just one option among many, equal to all others: it is the best kind of life for a human being to live. In fact, Socrates thought it to be so crucial to our being human that he concluded, 'The unexamined life is not worth living.'

Of course, the sky will not fall if we fail to meet that standard. But we should at least recognise what is at stake if we make the choice not to take up reflective, or mindful, practice.

FOUR IMPORTANT PHILOSOPHICAL TRADITIONS

Four important philosophical traditions have dominated Western-style thinking about ethics in the past three millennia. Although there are complexities associated with each of them, the basic ideas are easy to grasp, especially if some of the technical language is avoided.

- *Consequentialism.* If you ask people gathered in a room what they think should be done in a particular situation, about half of them will respond with a question: 'Well, what will happen if we choose option a, or b?' In asking about the likely consequences of a potential course of action, people hope to be able to do a kind of cost–benefit analysis so they can pick the option that achieves the greatest good or at least causes minimal harm.

  Throughout history, philosophers have offered different theories about what counts as 'good' or 'harm'. The most famous form of consequentialism, Utilitarianism, originally proposed that good equals pleasure and bad equals pain. Modern Utilitarians link the concept of 'good' to the realisation of preferences and that of 'bad' to aversions. What they share in common is a commitment to the strict equality of all persons. That is, they think that no individual's pleasure (or preferences) should count for more than another's.

  Consequentialists also think that it is possible, in principle, to compare options by calculating relative outcomes. For each option, you add up all the good that might be done and then subtract all the bad. Whatever option ends up with the highest positive score is the one you should choose.

- *Duty.* Opposing the view that consequences matter most is the view that we should act according to our duty, without considering

31

consequences, which on this view are irrelevant if one is acting ethically. People preferring this approach—about a third of the population in a country such as Australia—feel bound to honour promises, give effect to commandments (as from god) or, in the most sophisticated philosophical account (as advanced by Immanuel Kant), act in compliance with universally applicable maxims we prescribe for ourselves.

Kant's argument is based on the belief that human beings have an intrinsic dignity—largely based on our capacity to reason. As a result, no person may be used simply as the tool of another. Instead, we are bound by reason to comply with commandments we give ourselves and to do so regardless of the consequences and wholly as a matter of duty. For example, Kant argues that it is always wrong to lie or to break a promise. The 'wrongness' of lying has nothing to do with the outcome. Instead, Kant argues that we are bound to propose rules that can apply to all people, in all places, at all times. Such rules must be logically consistent, since any contradiction is inconsistent with the demands of reason. It is on that basis that Kant argues that lying is wrong: you cannot wish that everybody be free to lie while maintaining a basis for distinguishing between truth and falsehood. So, to wish that everybody be free to lie is to defy reason. And, for Kant, that's not on.

× *Virtue.* The third broad tradition is based on the idea that our individual and organisational characters are shaped by the choices we make. Adherents of this view do not want to know what the general consequences of a potential course of action will be. Nor are they concerned about duty for duty's sake. Faced with an ethical question, those inclined to virtue—slightly less than a fifth of people on average—will want to know the possible effects of one option or another on their character. Such people see their character as being like wax; that is, able to absorb the imprint of whatever touches it. Looking to Aristotle for inspiration, they believe that who you become is shaped by what you do.

- *Relativism*. The fourth approach is sceptical about the claim that any single approach to ethics can assume a special kind of legitimacy. In its 'strongest form' relativism says there are no absolutes—in knowledge, ethics, and so on. Thus, a relativist will claim that it is wrong to judge the ethics of others since only they are qualified to form a view of their conduct from 'within their own skin'. It is this idea that is often associated with the expression, 'When in Rome do as the Romans do.' At their best, relativists draw attention to the way in which powerful people and institutions are able to 'construct' ethical systems in their own image. That is, relativists invite a critical approach to ethical systems and a focus on the way those systems evolve throughout history. At their worst, relativists make strong, self-contradictory claims such as that, 'it is true that there is no such thing as "truth"' or, 'it is wrong to judge the conduct of others.'

Each of these four traditions has its strengths and weaknesses—often revealed in crude forms that the traditions' more sophisticated adherents would not support. Consequentialists can be led to advocate terrible injustices to a few innocent people if this will result in the realisation of enough 'good'. Those focusing on duty can also appear indifferent to great harms caused by complying with logically consistent (or divinely received) commandments. Those concerned with virtue can seem to value the shape of their character to the detriment of the welfare of others. And the power of relativists' analysis of the role of power is often overlooked because it is so easy to poke holes in the strong forms of their arguments.

It is easy to set up as 'straw men' mere caricatures of each tradition. Yet the broad brush strokes of each position are worth noting. The various positions are often appealed to in public debate. For example, scientists supporting the use (or destruction) of embryos in medical research often 'talk straight past' people raising religious objections to such practices. The former will be offering justifications based on consequences; the latter will be appealing to commandments from their god. There is little chance of either side really hearing the other—and little chance of real interaction.

Advocates for each tradition often present their approach as being all-encompassing, as something to be chosen to the exclusion of all others. In practice, I do not think that things are so clear. For example, some actions will be consistent with duty, will build a good character and also generate the best outcomes. You will only recognise such options if you are willing to look at the world through more than one moral lens.

As you will see, I am not a relativist. I think human beings should live an examined life—that this is the best kind of life. I am therefore comfortable enough to say to those who think this is just an option that they are wrong.

As you read further, you might like to pause from time to time to consider your own reaction to the questions being examined. Few of us are all one thing or another: we tend to apply or be influenced by a mixture of the four main traditions. Usually, though, we will have a leaning in favour of one particular approach. Where do you lean? Does this position change from situation to situation? How does your position affect the choices you make?

A FURTHER OPTION

Of late I have been wondering if it might be possible to combine some of the older traditions, as outlined, into a new synthesis that suits the times in which we live. Others have followed this path, but not quite in the direction I have been moving.

With that caveat in mind, I think there are interesting possibilities in an approach that integrates purpose, values and principles in a far more powerful form than is usually applied.

The central idea is simple and uncontroversial—that we should be accountable for the 'things' we make, in terms of both the 'what' and the 'how' of making. The 'things' to be made include physical artefacts, systems and institutions, as well as social artefacts such as families, communities and societies. The world, in fact.

Such an approach to ethics has a number of normative components. The things that are to be made should be 'fit for purpose'—as well as being coherent and complete. Things should also be made in the right way (the means must be appropriate to the ends). That is, the value of a 'thing' is not determined according to whether or not it produces a good outcome.

So, if we think of a building as an example of a thing to be made, it is not enough that it looks good. The thing made has to have been built with the right materials (say, good-quality cement and steel) and in the right way (adequate attention to the soundness of the work done) and with the right intentions, all of this forming part of what is made.

The ends (purposes) to be served should be constructive, not destructive. There is dignity in the role of being a 'maker'—whatever a person's particular level of skill—based on an appreciation of relative competence and creativity rather than criteria such as power, wealth and privilege. So, the class of 'makers' includes the artisans and artists as much as it does scientists, technologists, engineers and builders.

There is something very grounded about this approach to ethics, something that will make sense to people from all walks of life. It allows us to see our values and principles embodied in the things we make—and therefore in the world we help to fashion—in a particularly strong way. It calls on each person as a 'maker' to be responsible for the things they make, either as an individual or as part of a larger group.

I think this approach could be especially well placed to help people and society make better decisions in times of rapid and profound change (for example, in relation to new technologies) and in the reform of older institutions that need to adapt. It will draw us all back to questions of purpose, without necessarily demanding an abandonment of well-founded traditions. It could be something that can be embraced by progressives and conservatives alike.

There is much to be worked out here. There are many connections to older traditions (including that of Natural Law) to be explored. I think, however, that a new synthesis of the kind sketched here will be an essential ingredient in any response to the challenges we face now and in the future.

MOVING ON

By now you should have a general understanding of the field of ethics, its central question 'What ought one do?' and associated considerations. You should also be in a position to make at least a preliminary evaluation of your own ethical position in relation to purpose, values, principles and the scope of your circle of concern. You might have decided, if only tentatively, what constitutes your personal morality. And you might have a sense of your own appetite for living an ethical life, as opposed to a conventionally moral one.

All this will help you make better sense of the questions I explore in the body of this work—questions that arise as part of ordinary life. In discussing these things, I put forward what I think are relevant considerations—things to take into account. Much of what I say will reflect my own values and principles since the things I notice are the things I find important. You might notice different things, or you might think my point of view is odd or limited.

That is exactly as it should be. You should take everything I say with the proverbial grain of salt. Be sceptical. Ask yourself how my thoughts relate to your own ethical framework. But also be open to new ideas. Ask yourself if your response is based on certainties you have not really examined before. Are you bound to a moral code that is not yet your own but is simply inherited from the past as a result of the influence of parents, teachers, or others who have helped shape your life?

Finally, as you think about the questions I explore, consider what you might choose to do in practice and how this will not only reveal the unfolding shape of your life but also contribute to this world.

THE QUESTIONS

The topics considered in this section were selected from a long list of suggestions made by members of The Ethics Centre, people attending events such as the Festival of Dangerous Ideas, and colleagues and acquaintances.

The topics cover the full spectrum of 'seriousness'. Discussion of ethics should not be reserved for some special class of events; instead, the ethical dimension should be seen to engage us more generally—even in what might seem to be the most mundane aspects of our lives. That is why I chose to deal with concerns ranging from abortion to mobile phone etiquette—matters that would rarely be brought together in one list.

Much of what I have to say is likely to be a source of disagreement. Some entries might be dismissed as too flimsy or obvious. I am willing to court such criticism. This book is not intended to provide an authoritative guide to life's difficult (or easy) questions; the intention is to prompt reflection and discussion. Additionally, I am struck by how often what seems obvious to one person is a revelation to another.

In the future I might create an online site where people can add topics and propose their own account of what should be considered by others. In that sense this book is but a beginning.

A CITIZEN'S OBLIGATION TO GOVERNMENT

A government minister proudly told me every person was one of his 'customers'. He expected me to be pleased. I told him I was not a customer but instead I was a citizen. His response was to say that there is no practical difference.

In a democracy, citizens are the ultimate source of authority for all government power. Their relationship with government ministers is not defined by transactions. Their authority neither waxes nor wanes according to their use of government services. It is a fixed term in the equation of democratic political power.

Governments should exist to serve the interests of citizens, not merely to satisfy their wants. This requires that governments see the relationship in terms that are broader than those of purchaser and provider. In return, the duties of citizens are to obey the law (within the bounds of conscience), to contribute the means by which government might proceed (through the payment of taxes and tariffs), to participate in the processes of democratic deliberation (at a minimum by turning up to vote) and to be informed and enabled (through education and so on) so that they can contribute within the private sphere to the creation and maintenance of a good society.

The minister with whom I was speaking is a genuinely good man. He is sincere but mistaken: citizens are never simply the customers of government.

THE QUESTIONS

Governments seem to have all the power, and this can engender in them a sense of being in charge and therefore able to dictate the nature of their relationship with citizens. In a democracy this is an illusion. All authority comes ultimately from the citizens, since it is they who control the constitution on which all power is ultimately founded. What then is the citizen's obligation to government?

In particular:

× Do you have a sound understanding of the relationship between a government and its citizens?

× Do you do your part to deserve the honour of being a citizen?

× Do you seek to hold government to account for its use of power?

× Do you take the provision of good services to be the full extent of a government's duty to you as a citizen?

ABORTION

Abortion is one of those 'touchstone' subjects that can drive families and communities into deeply divided, even hostile, camps. My interest in abortion is personal. When I was a boy my mother faced the choice between grave health risks likely to result in her death and giving birth to my unborn brother. In a letter to her sister, she wrote:

> I had to go back to Dr [X] today and he has
> explained that unless the pregnancy is terminated
> it will mean the certain death of the baby and if not
> my own death then permanent damage resulting in
> my becoming a complete invalid.

> As you can imagine I am in a turmoil. I feel strongly
> that I couldn't live with myself were I to permit a
> termination and yet I must consider [my husband]
> and the three children I have. Also I wonder have I
> the right to virtually commit suicide?

I found this letter long after I had begun work at The Ethics Centre. One of my first tasks at The Centre had been to establish the Ethi-call service, a place my mother might have come to for help while wrestling with her dilemma. But this was all too late for her. In the end she chose to have the baby, and she died a year and a day later. She was, however, true to her conscience and at peace with her decision. My brother, Angus, lived.

Most decisions about abortion do not involve such a terrible choice between the life of a mother and that of an unborn child. For the most part, the question is squarely to do with the right of a woman to control her own body. It is undeniable that, for those who wish for it, pregnancy can be a rich and fulfilling experience. But to give over one's body in order to sustain another life must be a free choice. Otherwise the burden is unjust.

The principal objection to abortion comes from those who argue that a foetus, any foetus, has a right to life. This claim is often associated with a religious belief that all life is a gift from god and that humans have no right to take life—and certainly not an innocent life. Abortion is thus treated as a form of murder. This argument is relatively new: it used to be the case that a person did not exist until they were born. An unborn foetus might well be alive, but that does not mean it is a person, the term used to identify a being with the full range of moral rights and responsibilities. In fact, until relatively recently an unborn child could not be murdered because the law did not recognise them as a person. This is changing, although the law does allow exceptions.

There are good reasons, both scientific and theological, for rejecting the idea that a person comes into existence at the moment of conception. Although human life may begin at the moment the egg is fertilised, a number of days pass before the egg is implanted and the cells sufficiently differentiated to establish some kind of identity. That is, there is a period when it is impossible to ascribe 'personhood' to an embryo. From a theological perspective, given the precarious circumstances of a newly fertilised ovum, it would be a cruel and pointless act for an omnipotent and omniscient being to plant a soul in an embryo that it knows is destined to succumb. There does, however, come a point in a pregnancy when the embryo grows into a foetus with an increasing chance of assuming an identity and sustaining life. This is where the practical choices become difficult.

It is possible to test what people really think about this subject by running a 'thought experiment'. Philosopher and educator Dr Leslie Cannold did this as part of her doctoral research.[5] She worked with a number of women who identified themselves as either 'pro-life' or 'pro-choice', asking them to imagine that a baby could be grown in an artificial womb, using a process called 'ectogenesis', and whether they would approve of the process. The assumption was that women on both sides of the debate would say yes. The pro-life women would get what they said they wanted—preservation of the life of the unborn child. The pro-choice women would get what they said they wanted—control over their bodies. As it turned out, both groups of women refused to give their approval.

Dr Cannold found that many of the pro-life women did not merely want the unborn child to live: they also wanted the pregnant woman to 'accept responsibility' and live through the consequences of becoming pregnant. The pro-choice women did not merely refuse

---

5 Cannold, L (n. d.), 'The Abortion Myth', http://cannold.com/articles/article/the-abortion-myth/.

to bear an unwanted child, they also insisted that no other person become the parent of the child that would otherwise be born. In other words, advocates for both sides of the argument about the ethical status of abortion harboured reasons other than the ones publicly stated. As is often the case with such matters, it is important to look below the surface arguments to find what is really driving the debate.

Finally, it would be wrong to assume that women are typically distressed by the prospect of having an abortion. Many report leaving the clinic feeling happy, relieved and in charge of their lives. They are not in grief.

Ultimately, the decision whether or not to proceed with an abortion should be solely that of the woman—acting in accordance with a well-informed conscience. The decision bears on her more than on any other person and must be hers to make. That was the approach my father took. He recognised that it was ultimately my mother's right to decide.

THE QUESTIONS

Does a woman's right to control her own body take precedence over the life of a foetus that, undisturbed, will be born a human child?

In particular:

× Is there someone trustworthy and disinterested you can turn to for guidance?

× At what stage in the pregnancy is the decision being made? The earlier the decision is made the less likely it is that the embryo will have developed to the point where it can assume a separate identity. (As noted, some religions, such as Roman Catholicism, do not believe that a soul is automatically inserted into each growing child. In this case it is hard to understand why an omniscient, omnipotent and benevolent god would place a soul in a being known to have no future.)

* Are you under any pressure either to terminate the pregnancy or to keep the child?

* Does anyone else have a legitimate right to be consulted as part of your decision-making?

* Will you be able to live with your decision? Answering yes will not lessen the emotional burden you will feel, but in the long run knowing you have made what, for you, is the right decision will sustain you.

ADOPTION

Some couples are unable to conceive and bear children of their own. This might be for reasons such as problems with fertility or it might be a consequence of family structure — especially the case for same-sex couples who do not have children from other relationships. In all cases, among the available options are sperm and egg donation, surrogacy, and the use of assisted reproductive technologies. Another option, however, is to seek to adopt a child born of other parents who are unable or unwilling to care for them. In most countries the process of adoption is carefully regulated, the primary aim being to ensure the long-term welfare of the children. This involves careful assessment of the suitability of potential adopting parents — whether they have the means to support a family and also in terms of the character of each individual and the nature of their relationship.

In recent times the rights of adopted children have expanded to include a right to seek contact with their biological parents, although this right is rarely exercised against the will of the adopting parents. People are often very keen to learn about their origins and, if possible, to find biologically related siblings and members of their extended family. Finding out about one's medical history can often be a strong motivation too.

In practice, though, the most significant practical concerns facing adopting parents are to do with determining the number of children to be adopted, making decisions about breaking up natural pairings (brothers and sisters in an orphanage, say) and working out when and how to let a child know they are adopted.

In general, the older children become the more interested they will be in their origins and the more conscious they will become of perceived differences in the way they look. The welfare of an adopted child is usually best secured if the adoptive parents are honest and direct with them from the time they start asking questions. Ideally, these parents will know something of the child's biological parents, and this information, along with small details and memorabilia from the child's life before and after adoption, can be collected in a 'life book'—something that provides continuity in the child's life narrative. Naturally enough, discovering that one is adopted can give rise to many emotions: these should be allowed to flow, always remembering that the child will feel safe in the love and home of their adoptive parents, who specifically chose them above all others.

Then, of course, there is the fate of the children nobody chooses to adopt. They might not be attractive or appealing; they might have a troublesome nature. Even so, they would no doubt also hope to find a home beyond their orphanage. If you participate in the adoption system in order to find a child of your own, what obligation, if any, might you have to those not fortunate enough to be selected? What must it feel like to always be left behind?

THE QUESTIONS

People seeking to adopt a child need to think hard about a variety of factors. Are they confident that the child has not been made available by unscrupulous means—for example, the exploitation of vulnerable biological parents or even theft? Are they sure they can offer a life that is at least as good as, if not better than, the life the child would have if not adopted? Do they have the capacity to provide a stable family life in which the adopted child can flourish?

In particular:

* Do you have the quality of relationship, and the means, to enable you to adopt and nurture a child?

* Will you be in a position to explain to your adopted child details of their origin, consistent with your duty to respect the privacy of the biological parents?

* How do you balance the interests of all the children who are available for adoption against your desire to make a family? What obligation, if any, do you have to those you leave behind because they do not fit your vision of the 'ideal child'?

AGEING

With the shameful exception of Aboriginal and Torres Strait Islander peoples, the average lifespan of most Australians is increasing. The latest prediction is that by 2056 in New South Wales the average lifespan for a woman will be 91.4 years and that for a man will be 85.0 years.[6] This extension of life is dramatic: as recently as 2007 to 2009 average life expectancy was 83.9 years for newborn females and 79.3 years for newborn males.[7] At the same time, advances in medicine and related technologies (prostheses, genetics and so on) are increasing the likelihood not only of living longer lives but also of living healthier ones.

Yet for the most part our working and social arrangements remain attuned to a time when the majority of men would die not long after retiring at the age of sixty-five. The result of this very important demographic change is that an increasing number of Australians now need to re-imagine how they should live for more than twenty years after retirement, at a time when they might be old but are not necessarily aged and frail.

When some people reach retirement age they are exhausted by their work. This is often the case for people who have derived their income from manual labour in factories, on farms and so on. Such people can see the enjoyment of some rest and leisure as the holy grail. Others might want or need to continue working, either as a matter of choice or through financial necessity. Governments are already planning to raise the age of retirement to seventy-two, mostly in order to help fund the increasing costs of aged care.

People such as Marc Freedman, founder and CEO of Encore.org, are now suggesting that we need to create a new category of life for

6 New South Wales Treasury, http://www.treasury.nsw.gov.au/__data/assets/pdf_file/0016/128131/NSW_Treasury_-_Intergenerational_Report_2016_web.pdf.

7 Australian Bureau of Statistics, http://www.abs.gov.au/AUSSTATS/abs@.nsf/Lookup/4102.0Main+Features10Mar+2011.

this period,[8] much as psychologist and educator Granville Stanley Hall created the category of 'adolescent' in the late 1800s and early 1900s.[9] Freedman has proposed that we consider the time between middle and old age as a time of opportunity to find meaning in a life that is no longer defined by family commitments or economic necessity. My friend Alan Schwartz described his thinking to me in a personal email:

> ... Today I can reasonably expect another 20 strong and healthy years. How will I (and millions of my generation) navigate these newly minted, un-named and uncharted years? I feel that the right answer is something like this: 'In order to live the next 20 years fulfilled and happy I must, with great focus and urgency, redirect my experience and resources towards projects for the benefit of future generations.'
>
> This is far easier said than done. I fear that not only I but a significant proportion of my fellow travellers will not achieve their potential. Without the support of rites, routes and social norms, too many of us may waste these bonus years. Too many of us may feel dislocated, unproductive and unfulfilled.

---

8 Marc Freedman (2012), *The Big Shift: navigating the new stage beyond midlife*, http://www.amazon.com/Big-Shift-Navigating-Beyond-Midlife/dp/1610390997.

9 Wikipedia (2017), 'Stanley Hall', https://en.wikipedia.org/wiki/G._Stanley_Hall.

> Whilst this is a personal tragedy for each lost person, it is also a lost opportunity for society. To avoid the waste and to harness the potential of this new age we must, with great urgency, invent, design and propagate the *rites, routes* and *social norms* for this new age ...[10]

Of course, not everyone will be free to make these choices. Some will be committed to the task of caring for loved ones; some will lack the financial resources to look much beyond day-to-day survival; and many will be denied the opportunity to do as they would like simply because they are sick or frail.

What we make of all this will vary from individual to individual. The central point is that there are new options to be considered and, therefore, choices to be made.

THE QUESTIONS

As we live longer, in better health, what might we do with the additional years once we are free of other obligations? Do we relax into old age or look for new sources of meaning—perhaps defining new pathways for growth?

In particular:

- What value do you attach to the extra years of life you hope to enjoy?

- To what extent does uncertainty about the future shape your choices?

---

10 Alan Schwartz, pers. comm., May 2016.

⨯ Are you bound by duties that must take precedence over your own interests?

⨯ Who else might be affected by your decisions? What might they think about your choices?

⨯ Have you done enough? Is it now time to rest and play?

⨯ What are the institutional and cultural barriers that might limit your choices? Do you have the time and energy to challenge and change these things?

⨯ How do you ensure that others can have the same choices as those you are contemplating? Are you just in a privileged position—a position denied others?

ALCOHOL

I have had some unfortunate encounters with alcohol—those nasty hangovers that make you say to yourself, 'Never again.' For all that, though, I still enjoy an occasional drink—in moderation, of course.

It is undeniable that, despite its availability and widespread acceptance in society, alcohol is a dangerous drug. It fuels preventable violence; it turns otherwise sensible people into fools; and it can cause long-term health problems that are a burden not only for the affected individuals but also for society.

We all carry the cost to families, the health system, the economy and so on. In recognition of these costs, from time to time some societies have sought to prohibit the manufacture and consumption of alcohol. Rarely has this worked—if ever completely. This might be in part because, taken in moderation, alcohol can also ease social tensions and expand horizons, one reason for its continuing popularity among a large range of recreational drugs. Alcohol is also a 'cultural artefact', in that exceptional skill can be required to make it well. Natural products (such as fruit, grains and water) are transformed into remarkable new products that not only intoxicate but also delight the senses.

The greatest criticism of alcohol usually comes from those who denounce its tendency to degrade the human capacity for reason, thus separating us from the 'divine' (in religious terms) or removing our control over our basest instincts. Yet some religions incorporate alcohol in their rituals—for Christians, for example, Christ's first miracle is believed to have been turning water into wine—and others embrace the 'loosening' of reason as an opportunity to feel more deeply.

THE QUESTIONS

Can alcohol be consumed with a degree of moderation that allows its benefits to be experienced while minimising or eliminating its costs?

In particular:

× Is this a safe place to drink alcohol—a safe location, in the company of sensible people, at the right time, and so on?

× Are you at the point where drinking more will not improve your experience and instead probably just make you sick?

× Are others being adversely affected by your intoxication? Do they have a right not to be affected by you in this situation? Are you being sensitive to their cultural or religious values?

× Do you have any back-up plans—safe transport, food, accommodation and so on?

× Do you have a right to offer others alcohol? Are there children involved and, if so, what formal and informal 'rules' apply?

ANIMAL WELFARE

When we enter a dark room most of us flick on the light without giving any thought to the extensive networks of people and equipment that lie behind the generation and distribution of electricity. The same thing applies to most of the food we consume: we typically spare little thought for the farmers and graziers, the truckies, the processors and so on, who are responsible for feeding us.

The people involved in our food supply usually have the opportunity to speak out. We hear their voices from time to time—when there are natural disasters, for example, when monopolies seek to pay less than the cost of production, or when cheap imports flood the market. But animals cannot speak out: they depend on humans being willing to take up their cause and argue on their behalf.

Human attitudes to animals have varied considerably over time and according to differences in place and culture. Many indigenous peoples have kinship relationships with animals (and plants), and this network of relationships governs their interaction with animals. For example, it is often taboo for a human related to an animal to kill it. Others will be allowed to kill it, but the person with the direct kinship relationship must not. Even then, the person doing the killing might act with a sense of deep reverence for the life being taken. This can lead to moments of ritual and spiritual recognition of the animal's 'gift' of life and a care and concern that this gift not be wasted. As a consequence, those involved will often make use of all the animal's body can offer.

Modern Western societies tend to have lost this sense of reverence — especially when it comes to animals farmed on an industrial scale. Individual farmers and graziers often develop strong emotional connections with their animals, even when they know they are destined for slaughter, but the ultimate consumers barely give the animals a thought or, if they do, think of them as just another commodity to be transformed for their use. Personal affection for animals is instead reserved for pets, which are often specially bred to appeal to their human owners. This has resulted in animals shaped in ways that nature never intended, often causing them to suffer. For example, British bulldogs have been bred to have heads so large as to make it impossible for a bitch to deliver her own pups by natural means. There are many other examples.

Professor Peter Singer is Australia's most influential philosopher. His thinking and his lifestyle have had enormous influence throughout the world—especially in relation to how humans should think about and relate to animals. His starting point is that animals can experience both pleasure and pain, to a degree that is, in principle, indistinguishable from our own capacity. He argues that as a consequence we should relate to animals with as much care as possible. He further argues that most of the pain animals suffer for the sake of humans is unnecessary—that humanity could be clothed, fed and entertained by means that cause no harm to animals. In keeping with this, Singer is a vegan to the extent that the circumstances of his working life allow. Although he makes use of medicines tested on animals, he urges that these 'animal models' be replaced by other means of testing as soon as possible and that humanity make active plans to do this rather than waiting until the technology emerges.

Activists' ability to expose instances of animal cruelty and exploitation has prompted a new and growing community awareness of the plight of animals. Animal welfare has not yet acquired overriding importance in the public mind, but there is certainly a trend in favour of products that are produced with a consciousness of animal welfare. Hence the increasing sales of free-range eggs—a term that is now defined, albeit not as most people in the community would assume. Based on a compromise with industry, the definition allows chooks to be kept in crowded barns and not, as some might expect, roaming free outdoors.

The community has broadly accepted the simple proposition that if animals are to be used for the benefit of humanity they should live well and die well. The ideal of a 'good life' for an animal is a life lived as close to the animal's natural existence as possible, one in which it can realise its nature in a suitable environment before dying free of pain or distress. Most (perhaps all) pigs love to wallow in mud: to lock a pig in a concrete stall for its entire life is to deny it the opportunity to live in its natural state of pig-ness.

Opposed to the realisation of this ideal, however, is the reality of economics. In general, to raise animals with care and compassion is more expensive than the cheaper alternative of mass farming. My observation is that most farmers and graziers would much prefer to improve their animals' quality of life. But that would mean the community had to pay more for food, and so far this is not what the majority of people demand. It is certainly not wanted by the intermediaries, those large corporate entities that are motivated primarily by market conditions and the desire to maximise their profits and their return to shareholders.

Making things even more difficult is the fact that the debate about animal welfare is not just about pleasure, pain and suffering. Some philosophers, such as Peter Singer, make a larger claim—that some animals (primates, higher mammals and so on) are 'persons', that some animals fall into the same ethical category as human beings, and that it is therefore wrong to use animals merely as a means towards the satisfaction of our ends.

The argument is directly comparable with that used to bring about the end of slavery. It was argued then that slaves are persons, with intrinsic dignity, and therefore could not be the property of others. It was not that slavery was cruel (although it often was); rather, slavery was condemned as a violation of each person's fundamental right to liberty and respect. Advocates of animal rights are calling for a similar examination of the status of animals. Are they human property? Or are some of them, at least, to be considered 'persons'?

Some people vehemently object to the idea of animals being elevated to the ethical status of humans. Often these objections have their basis in religion: only 'man' was made in the image of god. Others arise from scepticism about animals' ability to make conscious ethical choices that take them beyond the dictates of instinct and desire.

In the end, animals and humans are made of the same stuff. All cling to life; all are open to pleasure and susceptible to pain. That much would seem obvious. So, even if we might argue about animals' 'personhood', there is much to be considered when it comes to their welfare, whether they are domesticated or wild, whether they are used for food or other goods that humans want or need.

THE QUESTIONS

How should we think about and treat animals? What is the extent of our individual and collective obligation, in general, to ensure their welfare?

In particular:

- Are there suitable alternatives to using animals to provide the things we need or want?

- Are our choices sensitive to the effects they might have on animals, for better or for worse?

- Do we have reliable information about how animals have been treated in the production of what we buy?

- Are we paying enough to farmers and graziers so that their animals might live well and die well—as most rural producers would prefer?

- Should we recognise 'animal rights'?

- Where do we draw the line with animals: should we care about an ant in the way we might care about a cat or a dog?

- Does the existence of pain and suffering experienced by animals in the natural world relieve humans of the obligation to reduce pain and suffering for animals living under our control?

ANIMALS AND PRODUCT TESTING

Many people owe their health and wellbeing, and perhaps even their survival, to the fact that animals have been used to test break-throughs in medicine. There are also many people whose vanity or comfort is thanks to animals that have been tested on to ensure that products such as shampoos and cosmetics can be used without irritation or other harm. Animals are the 'bunnies' in both cases, so how are we to determine the boundaries of what is acceptable?

Some people argue that animals should never be tested on for any purpose and that if we want to know what is good or bad for humans we should test products and formulations on humans—not rats, primates and so on. Their argument is not only that humans are a more suitable 'test subject' but also that if we humans are to be the beneficiaries of such research we should also bear its cost.

At the other extreme there are people who think of animals as living objects that humans can own and that we should be able to use them as we please. The argument here holds that animals are just another tool to be used for human progress and wellbeing. It does not necessarily follow from this that people may be cruel to animals, but if there has to be a choice between human suffering and animal suffering then it is the suffering of animals that is the lesser evil.

Then there are people in the middle of the two extremes, typically accepting that there are some important human 'goods' (such as medicine) that will advance only if animals are tested and hoping that a better alternative can be found as soon as possible. These people might agree to animal testing for essential purposes, but they are far less likely to accept it for 'optional extras' such as in connection with cosmetics.

Finally, there are the scientists and technologists who develop and use animal testing techniques. For the most part, their work is tightly regulated, the focus being on minimising suffering and maximising the good of the animal. Historically, animals were often subjected to cruel procedures, but today most animals are treated with care and used only when there is no alternative.

THE QUESTIONS

Under what circumstances should animals be used for testing? Are there any situations in which you would refuse to use a product derived from animal testing?

In particular:

× Is the product that has been tested on animals essential—for example, to develop a life-saving medicine—or are animals being tested simply as a matter of human convenience?

× How would you feel if the life of your child or another family member was at stake?

× Would you be willing to be the guinea pig for testing if animals are not to be used?

× If you have a pet would you allow it to be tested?

× Have the people testing animals exhausted all other alternatives?

× Do you know whether animals have been used for testing in the creation of your product? Would you stop buying a particular product if you found out it had been tested on animals?

× Are you familiar with the rules and regulations governing the use of animals in scientific research?

× How can we ensure that animals have a voice, so that they are not left to suffer unnecessarily and in silence?

APPROACHING DEATH

The possibility of death is part of life. Our death, the death of loved ones—these are things to which we must eventually turn our mind, no matter how distasteful the idea is.

Attitudes to death vary according to cultures and times, but one unifying principle appears again and again, regardless of context. This is that a 'good death' is the ultimate expression of a 'good life'.

So it is that Viking warriors would hope their final moment might be spent on the field of battle, with sword, axe and shield in hand against a foe. Religious martyrs would count it a good death if they were living their faith to the end. (This approach also explains some of the gruesome aspects of capital punishment in societies that believe a bad life should end in a bad death.)

Most people would never deem a violent death a good death; instead, the hope would be for a death free of suffering and distress. Again, the idea of a good life presses in. If the final moments of life are to be easy, there should be no regrets for things done badly. This need not be out of fear of some afterlife punishment: it might simply be that at the end there is little or no opportunity to make good the wrongs you have done to others.

Of course, some people are indifferent to the wellbeing of others. Many live and die quite content in the knowledge that they have acted without regard for the feelings or welfare of other people— without guilt, without remorse. There is in this world no moral economy in which the virtuous are rewarded and the wicked punished. In northern Namibia and southern Angola, the Himba people mark the life of each person through song. Every event of significance in a person's life is incorporated in a song that grows over their lifetime. The final singing of the song takes place when members of the tribe gather around the dying person.[11] These people approach death listening to the retelling of their life—all that was good and all that was bad. How then could one have a good death if one had not lived a good life?

The other aspect of death concerns not us but others. From time to time we might be required to make decisions about the continuation or withdrawal of medical treatment. It is to be hoped that a person whose life hangs in the balance will have made their wishes clear, but often this is not the case. At such times it is essential that a crucial distinction be kept in mind—the distinction between prolonging life and prolonging the process of dying. Without knowing it, we can sometimes become complicit in decisions that make our loved ones die a lingering death. Medical technology cannot make such ethical distinctions. We can.

THE QUESTIONS

We are all destined to die, as are our loved ones. What should be our attitude to the transition from life to death, the natural conclusion to every life?

In particular:

× What basic values and principles do you think define a 'good life'? To what extent do you uphold these values and principles in practice?

---

11 https://www.facebook.com/TheMindUnleashed/photos

- Do you live without regrets? How would you feel if your life, in its entirety, were to be sung to you as you die—with you having no further chance to make good the wrongs you have done?

- Do you take solace from a belief that there might be justice in a life to come? Or does that idea terrify you?

- Can you accept death as a natural part of life, rather than as something separate from life?

- Are we able to distinguish between prolonging life and prolonging the process of dying, especially when it really counts?

ATTENDING BORING EVENTS

People are sometimes invited to events they would probably prefer to avoid. In many cases their presence (or absence) will not be noticed because they are just there to make up the numbers. In other cases you can reliably predict that the occasion will be memorable only for how bad it is, yet there is an expectation that you will go for the sake of others for whom your showing up really matters.

Then again, plenty of people have attended an event with the greatest reluctance only to be pleasantly surprised. If they had given in to their immediate preference, without regard for others, they would have missed out on one of the best occasions of their life— new opportunities, a new romance, new friends, etcetera, etcetera.

THE QUESTIONS

Life is short, so why spend time doing something that experience tells you will be tedious? Why let the interests of others take precedence over your own likes and dislikes?

In particular:

- Have you wondered whether your expectations might be based on false assumptions? Could the event be better than anticipated?

- Are there things you could do to improve the experience—for example, go with a friend?

- Do you have a special commitment that could be honoured through your attendance—for example, an obligation because of a family connection?

- Do you *really* have a better alternative?

- Have you considered that one of the costs of being part of society is a requirement to socialise with different types of people at times when you might prefer to be alone or elsewhere?

BECOMING A POLITICIAN

One of a citizen's noblest aspirations used to be to play a role in the political life of their society and in so doing help to 'make a difference' in the world. These days, however, politicians tend to be vilified or at least sneered at.

Many people seeking election now come from the major political parties, being drawn from the ranks of ministerial advisers and union and party officials. That is, most are already members of the political class. This—along with some of the more dubious actions of political parties, as private associations in the pursuit of public power—has brought politicians' stocks low. Indeed, the whole political enterprise is increasingly open to question, at least in the liberal democracies of the West, and populist anti-politicians are in the ascendancy.

One response to the decline in the status of politics has been the emergence of new modes of citizen involvement—including the use of citizen juries, whereby ordinary people can make informed decisions about matters of public policy. There are, however, other options, among them the possibility that a wider cross-section of the community might make themselves available to serve as elected representatives. Those who do will have to make sacrifices, especially of time with family and friends. Politics is a demanding profession. But we citizens have few grounds for complaint if we are not willing to serve.

THE QUESTIONS

If politics is failing the community, do we have an obligation to become part of the solution? Is it reasonable to expect people from outside the political class to volunteer for a period of civic service?

In particular:

- Are you willing to accept the consequences of not being involved in your nation's political life?

- Are the costs in terms of family and personal life too high?

- Are there other ways of making a difference—other than seeking elected office?

- Do you have a clear idea of what would make for a good society should you be given the opportunity to shape the future?

BLENDED FAMILIES

Blended families are becoming the norm, separated and divorced individuals finding new partners and being willing to accept and integrate the children born of past relationships. It is not always plain sailing, though. There are, for example, widely acknowledged problems faced by stepmothers. But it can go further than this, as in the case of a divorced father whose daughter asked him not to bring his new partner to her twenty-first birthday party.

Scientific advances in the area of assisted reproduction—along with greater public acceptance of the fact that same-sex couples can love each other with at least the fidelity of heterosexual couples—have led to a new frontier in family formation, whereby same-sex couples form stable families with children that have been conceived and delivered by one of the parents or a surrogate, or have been adopted.

THE QUESTIONS

How should you respond when one part of the family rejects another part—for example, if a child from an earlier marriage refuses to acknowledge their parent's new partner or a new step-sibling? What if relatives refuse to acknowledge the legitimacy of the new blended family unit, perhaps for religious or cultural reasons that might, say, oppose divorce?

In particular:

× Do you have a right to impose your ethical standards on others?

× If the variation from your standard is a consequence of features in a person's life over which they have no control—for example, sexual orientation is rarely if ever something that people choose—is it fair to take this into account when assessing their family arrangements?

× Who bears the costs and derives the benefits of particular family arrangements?

× Do you recognise a hierarchy of duties in relation to the blended family structure? Is blood really thicker than water?

× Are the wishes of children who live under the control and influence of parents deserving of more consideration because they lack effective choice when it comes to family structure?

× Can a compromise be reached in the case of, say, a daughter refusing her father permission to bring his new partner to her party? For example, demeaning as it could be, might it be agreed that the new partner can come to some but not all of the party? If compromise is not possible, does either person have a stronger case? For example, if it is the daughter's celebration might she reasonably expect her preferences to be afforded precedence?

BREAKING THE LAW

The rule of law is one of the founding principles for life in Australia. It is based on rejection of the alternative principle that 'might makes right', which over millennia has been used by thugs and bullies to justify their exploitation of the relatively weak. Some of these thugs and bullies had grand titles and aristocratic antecedents; some subsequently decided to try to atone and do some good in the world, often because they feared punishment in the hereafter. No matter how one might dress up the brutality, though, the use of violence and oppression was stark and burdensome.

In principle, the rule of law insists that every person is equal before the law. No matter how mighty or wealthy, how weak or poor—all are supposed to be afforded justice without fear or favour. That is the ideal. We know the reality can be different, but it is hard to dismiss the principle. There is a presumption that we will all act lawfully.

Criminals place themselves outside this social compact, choosing to be outlaws, or outside the law. In earlier times outlaws could be killed with impunity: having decided to prey on others, they forfeited their liberties and rights. These days, and with a few rare exceptions (such as self-defence), individual citizens are not allowed to take the law into their own hands. That function is for the state, through the work of police forces, the courts and the penal system.

But not every person who breaks the law intends to harm their fellow citizens and society. Some feel that in all good conscience they cannot obey the law, most often because they believe the law to be unjust. Typically, these 'conscientious objectors' are willing to pay a price for their principled disobedience. Among them are people who refuse to serve in the military, who disrupt what they perceive to be environmentally damaging projects, who liberate animals suffering harm and who march in protest despite being ordered not to.

Sometimes, however, the form of protest imposes costs on others who are otherwise acting lawfully—for example, mining consortiums suffering a loss of production and timber workers losing their livelihoods. A true conscientious objector will be willing to make good those losses, even if they think they are linked to unethical conduct, and will be willing to pay the public cost of their principled but unlawful behaviour.

This is where the jury system comes in. It is always open to us to refuse to convict someone who has been accused of breaking the law—a privilege of citizenship that is all the more valuable for the rarity of its use.

THE QUESTIONS

Some laws are unjust. Some are foolish or have unforeseen consequences. Yet our society depends for its liberty, peace and security on the rule of law. Since all citizens benefit from this state of affairs, when might it be acceptable for a good citizen (as opposed to a criminal) to break the law as a matter of principle? And what should be the penalty for doing so?

In particular:

* Is your opposition to the law in question based on principle or personal convenience?
* Are you willing to accept the cost of your principled disobedience—including making good the loss your actions might cause others?
* What if everybody acted according to their own principles? Would this lead to anarchy?
* Are there lawful means by which you might be able to bring about the change you seek—for example, through law reform in parliament?
* Is unlawful conduct your first or last option?

BUSINESS ETHICS AND PERSONAL ETHICS

I know a man who is a devout practitioner of his religious faith. Yet in a candid moment he will speak of things he has done in business but would never do in his personal life. He explains the difference by saying it is not really him doing these things at work: he is just doing his job. There has long been debate about what might be the difference between the ethics of business and those of personal life. Some argue that the world of business is a kind of jungle in which there are no rules to govern survival. Others liken business to war — an obscene comparison if you know anything about the nature of war. The common approach, though, seems to be that the competitive nature of business brings with it a unique set of rules. Perhaps the most apt comparison lies with sport — where people compete within a framework of rules especially developed for the code in question.

Yet in both business and sport people make the rules and can choose whether or not to play. Additionally, the fact that a particular form of conduct is permitted does not necessarily mean one should engage in it. In the end we live just one life — ideally as an integrated whole. Our personal ethical framework might allow for a degree of flexibility in order to accommodate changing circumstances, but we need to know where the boundaries lie so as to avoid engaging in conduct that betrays our own idea of our better self.

In any case, businesses operate within the larger ethical context of the market, which cannot operate effectively and efficiently without a foundation of values and principles. Markets fail if participants lie, cheat or use power oppressively; such behaviours distort a market to a point where it is no longer free and therefore can no longer perform its proper role, which is to operate for the good of all.

Some people engage in work (espionage, for example) that requires them to behave dishonestly or unfairly as the cost of their striving for a greater good. This is known as the 'problem of dirty hands'.

The best that can be said of these instances is that they make sense or can be tolerated only if truly good people take them on for the sake of others and while being willing to bear the cost of doing so. Such circumstances are rare, usually arising in conditions of war or extreme public emergency.

I have never come across a case in business where the public good was such that compromising one's personal values could justifiably have been demanded. Businesses exist for private profit, even when they provide goods and services that are of benefit to individuals and the community. We might bend to suit the ethical requirements of an employer—but not to the point of breaking what lies at the core of our identity. To ask for that is to ask for too much when the primary aim is profit.

THE QUESTIONS

There are times—in business and at work more generally—when a person might be asked to apply an ethical standard that is contrary to their own. Is it reasonable to set aside personal ethics in such a situation? If context matters, should businesses be allowed to operate according to special ethical standards that would not be acceptable in general?

In particular:

× Should we treat businesses as a special ethical case in which the requirement to compete might excuse behaviour that would otherwise be considered unacceptable in civil society? Are businesses best understood as operating according to the law of the jungle, whereby the strong survive and the weak perish?

- Should businesses, and industry sectors, make clear the ethical foundations that shape the way they operate?

- Do you know where your own ethical boundaries lie? How far might you bend without breaking?

- Does working for a business organisation entail some adjustment to your own ethics when you are at work?

- Can you find an industry or employer with a reasonable 'fit' for your ethics?

BUSINESS ETHICS AND THE ENVIRONMENT

Every one of us has an opportunity to influence the world's response to climate change through the choices we make—most importantly, who we work for, buy from and invest in. For example, the choices we make in terms of such things as transport and travel, housing and appliances all have an environmental effect.

A number of eco-businesses have made a specialty out of offering goods and services that are environmentally sensitive. Those who do this well take into account not only the environmental footprint of their business but also the impact of the goods and services they produce and sell. Some companies can tell you precisely how much energy, carbon, water, and so on, is embedded in their product. They will know there is not much benefit in having a seriously green product if it is sold in, say, environmentally questionable packaging.

The central concern becomes one of transparency. Is a business that claims strong environmental credentials able to provide to you credible information with which to back up their claims, right across their supply chain? Further, is its approach based on a sound ethical foundation, or is it just a marketing gimmick of the moment? One can begin to answer this question only by looking at the business as a whole, across the full span of its relationships.

The main thing to think about here is that making a decision to work for, invest in or buy from a business on the basis of its environmental profile is just as legitimate as doing so because you like its logo. When it comes to the operation of free markets, ethical considerations are valid criteria, even if to say so ruffles the feathers of those who prefer to compete on more traditional grounds such as price. Ethics goes to the *value* of goods and services, not their price.

THE QUESTIONS

How can we choose businesses to deal with that are environmentally responsible?

In particular:

- Can the business offer clear and reliable evidence to support its environmental claims?

- Does the business take a comprehensive and integrated approach to the environment and its impact?

- Has this evidence been corroborated by an independent expert?

- Does the business report against internationally accepted standards such as those set by the Global Reporting Initiative?

- Can the business explain the connection between its environmental program and any additional costs you might be asked to bear? That is, are you confident that the business is not just marking up prices on the basis of spurious virtue?

⌅ Can you perceive a solid ethical foundation at work throughout the business as a whole?

BUYING LOCAL PRODUCTS

There are numerous reasons for preferring local providers of goods and services, among them the possibility of helping to preserve local jobs that sustain your community; having confidence in the standards used to create the products; reducing environmental impacts, with less energy consumed in transport; and obtaining a fresher product. On the other hand, buying local can also be more expensive, partly because additional costs might be incurred through factors such as higher wages and more stringent regulation.

More generally, a preference for local produce can disadvantage some of the world's poorest people, distant producers whose route out of poverty is based on hard work and access to open markets. They might be the people least able to afford the cost of your preference for 'home made'. Indeed, the whole system of global trade is based on the notion that the prosperity of all will be increased if we allow open markets within which goods and services are assessed on their merits and without prejudice.

THE QUESTIONS

There are some obvious advantages to buying locally produced goods and services, especially things such as food. But do our efforts to support local suppliers inadvertently harm people who have far more to lose and who are making their best effort to lift themselves out of poverty?

In particular:

- Are you aware of the impact of your choices on people you may never see or hear from?

- Does your decision to buy local secure the advantages you hope for? Or are you just falling victim to clever marketing? How might you find that out?

- Does the value of local purchasing pass through the entire supply chain—for example, back to the farm gate? Or are middlemen profiting from your choices and thus limiting the ethical benefits of your decisions?

BUYING ORGANIC PRODUCTS

For many people who want to obtain organic products, their choice is simply a matter of personal preference prompted by factors such as convictions about human health, flavour, the need to preserve species variety or even a desire to maintain traditional farming practices. For some, though, the choice arises from an ethical concern. This can be connected to disquiet about the use of pesticides and herbicides or genetically modified organisms, or it can involve a philosophical commitment to the preservation and extension of natural systems, environmental services and so on.

People who are sceptical about organic produce usually have two complaints. The first, a relatively minor concern, is that there seem to be multiple, and potentially unreliable, standards for what really counts as organic. A decent standard-setting process would resolve this problem. The more difficult complaint concerns the possibility that organic farming techniques can impose burdens on others who have not chosen this lifestyle—for example, through a failure to eradicate pests or the overuse of water (say, through the rejection of genetically modified plants that flourish with less).

THE QUESTIONS

How do I go about finding organic produce that can be relied on to meet an acceptable standard?

In particular:

x Does your purchase meet a credible standard for organic certification?

x Does the producer have a way of monitoring and rectifying any unintended consequences of production that might affect others?

x Will your purchase help make a real difference? Or is it tokenism?

x Is the good that you do in buying organic undone by your other actions—a bit like having two doughnuts after going to the gym?

x Do you even know whether you are buying organic? Some producers follow the principles without advertising the fact. They just think it makes a better product.

CHEATING

In Sydney's Martin Place, I sat with a small group of students who were about to sit their final exams. I asked them, just hypothetically, if they would make use of a leaked copy of the exam papers. Without hesitation they said they would. When I asked them why, they said, 'Isn't that what society teaches us? You do whatever it takes!' The odd thing was that these same students had moments before been telling me how they admired former Australian test cricketer Adam Gilchrist for his decision to surrender his wicket and walk when given not out during a World Cup semi-final.

I later encountered other students in a different location. They had been caught claiming the work of others as their own. Plagiarism is one of the worst things that can be done in academic circles, yet these students had no idea they had done something wrong. Instead, they belonged to a culture that perceived copying the words and ideas of a teacher to be a demonstration of the highest respect.

For many people the use of leaked exam papers or the copying of another person's work would be considered cheating. In essence, cheating involves dishonesty—especially of a kind that advantages an individual through deception—in that the cheat pretends to be playing by the rules when in fact they are not.

When asked about cheating, some people claim that honesty is a mug's game—'Everyone else is cheating, so you only hurt yourself by being honest.' Of course, not everyone else is cheating, but we get the point. In fact, the belief that others are not being honest can create a 'vicious spiral' in which confidence in the value of integrity is eroded. It is then that people start to redefine what cheating is. This can include approaches that ignore the spirit of the rules and instead look to the letter of the law—finding loopholes that technically allow behaviour that would otherwise be prevented.

Fortunes have been made by adopting this approach. This is probably what those students had in mind when they referred to the life lesson society had taught them: do whatever it takes.

THE QUESTIONS

Is it cheating if it is, strictly speaking, in accordance with the letter of the law? Is cheating allowable when others are already securing advantage by flouting the rules? Is cheating a commonly understood practice, or do we need to take account of cultural differences?

In particular:

× What rules apply in the context in which you are trying to decide whether to cheat?

× Would you be ashamed if your intended dishonest conduct became widely known?

× Are you comfortable with achieving success on the strength of a lie?

× Might a false success put others at risk? Imagine if your surgeon had cheated at university?

× Is it true that your success is put at risk by dishonesty on the part of others? If you know of this dishonesty, is your best, or only, strategy really to emulate their behaviour?

× What tactics could you employ that would allow you to be successful without compromising yourself?

CHILDREN AND DISCIPLINE

I am told my father sometimes came home thinking I had become infested with ringworms. As it happened, the tell-tale red rings on my legs were marks formed by the rounded edges of a wooden spoon my mother occasionally used for smacking me. That was pretty mild compared with punishments later meted out by others. I was 'slippered' at home, strapped and caned at school, and on one occasion scorched by a branding iron wielded by a relative after I had let a calf loose at the wrong time. As far as I can tell, exposure to corporal punishment did not scar me for life, either physically or psychologically.

But I never smacked my children. Not that they were unusually well behaved: they were not. Each was capable of stubborn, defiant naughtiness, but for the most part they were just being children — testing boundaries, and so on. Nevertheless, that didn't stop me from becoming so angry with my son on one occasion that I shouted at him, 'Stop behaving like a child!' 'But I *am* a child,' he replied. Which left me feeling completely deflated.

My wife's and my choice not to smack our children was not the result of a policy we had discussed and agreed on. It was just that other techniques seemed to work. For example, we would sometimes place a recalcitrant child in their bedroom, with the door closed but not locked. We also did things such as confiscate favourite toys and refuse access to treats.

Despite mounting evidence that smacking can be counter-productive, the law, throughout Australia, still allows a parent to smack their child using moderate force. Ideally, the smack is not meant to instil fear of the parent so much as to cause the child to recognise that wrongdoing has unpleasant consequences. Advocates of smacking argue that one of the greatest benefits is that the crime and the punishment are directly linked and that life can then proceed without any of the lingering resentment that can be associated with longer-term punishments such as confiscation and grounding. The main argument against smacking is that it normalises violence as a suitable response to wrongdoing. Research backs up the notion that smacking teaches the wrong lessons.[12]

Whatever you might think of the rights and wrongs of particular types of punishment, a few general principles should apply. First, the punishment should be proportional to the misdemeanour. Second, the process should always be fair, with like cases receiving a like response. Third, children need boundaries if they are to develop and maintain psychological health, so you do them no favour if there are neither rules nor consequences. Fourth, any use of force needs to be restrained and appropriate to the circumstances; punishments should never be meted out in anger. Finally, being patient and teaching your child to understand the basis for your rules and why they are sensible will usually deliver lifelong benefits; among other things, your children will be able to apply good and sensible rules while challenging those that are senseless and imposed through compulsion.

THE QUESTIONS

Have you considered how the way you set rules and deliver discipline will shape children's views about the relationship between justice and violence?

In particular:

× Have you informed yourself of the latest research results concerning the effectiveness of corporal punishment applied to children?

---

12 Australian Institute of Family Studies (2017), 'Publications', https://aifs.gov.au/cfca/publications/corporal-punishment-key-issues.

× Are you sure the rules you apply at home are fair and are understood by your children?

× Is your punishment suitably calibrated to your child's circumstances—age, gender, past experience, and so on? Is it fair to punish boys and girls in different ways and to a different degree?

× Are you cool-headed and restrained when deciding on and delivering punishments?

× Are you setting suitable boundaries for your children, considering the time and place in which they are growing up? Too many parents seek to replicate the circumstances of their own youth, but the world has changed.

× Are you respecting your children's dignity?

CHILDREN AND TECHNOLOGY

Humans have a tendency to flip between fear and enthusiasm in the face of new technologies. This is especially so when it comes to exposing children to these powerful forces for change. The reason is not hard to understand. Children are typically thought to be only partially formed by their limited life experience, so adults fear that exposure to damaging influences might leave a permanent scar on their child's development.

Precedents are easy to find. The widespread distribution of books after the invention of the printing press occasioned much alarm. Among other things, it was thought that children would be exposed to dangerous ideas, be distracted from useful activities such as work, and generally be at risk from a technology that even adults should be wary about. The concern was overstated, but something of its depth remains in the idea of the child bookworm—a child whose pleasure in reading might lead them to avoid games and other forms of physical development, who might spend all day in their room with their 'head in a book', failing to concern themselves with people and the world about them.

Sounds familiar? All you need to do is delete book and insert iPad, and the modern picture is complete.

Perhaps people were actually right to be worried about child bookworms, just as, perhaps, we should be worried about iPadworms. In general, one would think a child develops best when they encounter a broad repertoire of developmental experiences in the physical, psychological, social, spiritual and intellectual dimensions. But to argue a case for balance is very different from arguing that only one of the inputs (the digital one) is of its nature risky.

Perhaps the better question concerns what exactly is good for a child to encounter—whatever the platform. Returning to books, it is obvious that some books are not suitable for children. At the extreme are, say, pornographic texts, but other works might also be deemed inappropriate for children of certain ages. If one is to take this approach seriously, context will matter. For example, some fairy tales are extremely violent, yet their fantastic setting makes their lessons approachable without the risk of too much harm. The same might be said of stories contained in some religious texts or in epics such as Homer's *Iliad* and *Odyssey*. In short, the risks to children increase in proportion to the apparent proximity of the story to the 'real world' of their experience.

Online games and similar pastimes can be assessed in much the same way. Their appropriateness for any particular age group depends on context and on the latest evidence about how digital engagement might shape attitudes to real-life situations.

It should be noted that the need to make a prudent assessment will increase in line with the availability of virtual reality—a technology that seeks to blur, and eventually eliminate, the distinction between the simulated (digital) and the real (analog). While a child reading a book can protect themselves by toning down their imagination, a child experiencing virtual reality will be fully exposed. Unlike television or film—where there is a clear differentiation between story-telling and what is happening in the child's world—in cases of high-fidelity virtual reality, users' ability to calibrate their experience by tuning their imagination will be overridden by the programming decisions of the creators. That is a crucial difference.

THE QUESTIONS

How can parents ensure that their child's exposure to digital media is healthy and for their overall benefit?

In particular:

× What are your child's capacities and sensibilities?

× Are you using electronic devices as a kind of digital babysitter to keep your child occupied and quiet and relieve you from the task of continuous involvement?

× Are you able to monitor and, if necessary, control the digital content your child is gaining access to?

× Are you confident that the material your child is gaining access to is age appropriate?

× Have you taken into account the likely effect of virtual reality?

× Are you trying to ensure that your child is developing in a way that balances the physical, psychological, social, spiritual and intellectual dimensions in their life?

CHOOSING SCHOOLS

Education is the key to individual and societal wellbeing. In traditional societies it was usually a compulsory and lifelong obligation tied not just to survival but also to status. In most modern societies the form of education has changed: it is no longer based in community or clan groups but is instead offered by professional teachers within the formal institutional setting of schools. For all this difference, though, the quality of a person's education can still make a major difference to their life opportunities. This is not to suggest that education determines everything: some people live joyous, fulfilled lives of distinction having had very little formal education. Nevertheless, choosing a child's school is a decision of sufficient importance as to warrant serious consideration.

Some people will have relatively few options, perhaps because they have limited financial means or because they belong to a faith group that restricts their choices. If, however, a real choice is available, a number of factors should be taken into account:

× Does your child have special abilities or requirements that should be recognised and catered for? If so, what assurances can the school give you as to its having the necessary resources and skills? For example, will your child need access to special equipment or special teachers?

× Does your child need to attend a school that will socialise them in a manner that allows them to relate authentically to their community? (Such communities can be defined by religion or language or some other distinctive attribute.) In thinking about this, you might consider whether the necessary knowledge, skills and understanding might be obtained by means other than attending a special or exclusive school. For example, students often attend special weeknight or weekend classes in order to learn the language of their parents or, say, to receive special religious education while attending a general school.

× Whatever the particular circumstances of your child, family or community, there is something appealing about the idea of a common educational experience helping to bind all citizens together in a democratic society. This is the great promise of public education — that it becomes a unifying force in an otherwise disparate society.

× Schools vary considerably, not least in terms of their focus and character. These differences can affect not only students but also their parents. Some schools welcome parental engagement; others keep parents at a distance. And then there is the matter of location: some schools will be close to family and friends, whereas attending others will entail considerable time and effort.

In the end, the primary consideration concerns what is best in terms of the education of the child, who is seen not necessarily as an isolated individual but in the context of their family and community.

THE QUESTIONS

In choosing a school for your child, how do you balance the child's needs against family and wider social goods?

In particular:

× Have you fully considered the collective good to society of shared educational experiences?

- ✗ Does your child (or family) have genuine needs that differ from those of the majority and require special education?

- ✗ Is free choice of education a basic right in which others' interests are irrelevant?

- ✗ Where do the interests of your child stand in your calculation?

- ✗ Have you taken into account location and proximity to friends and family?

- ✗ Are the travelling obligations—including for extracurricular activities—reasonable?

- ✗ Will your child be recognised and cared for as an individual, or will he or she just be 'filling a place'?

- ✗ Will the school welcome and support your participation as a parent?

- ✗ Has the school a reputation for being fair to all its students, not just the 'stars'?

- ✗ Does the school support diversity among people and achievements?

CO-WORKERS AND LOYALTY

By definition, organisations are places of collective endeavour. Although some people might perform a specialist role, and be remunerated accordingly, there is a general expectation that everyone will make a reasonable effort to advance the organisation's interests. Things can become awkward if an individual or group fails to pull their weight. Or it can be even more serious. For example, some employees 'go rogue' and actively work against the interests of their organisation. They might steal, they might compromise vital business processes, they might undermine management; all of this being done furtively. Occasionally a fellow employee will realise what is happening: what then?

It used to be the case in Australia that a person never 'dobbed on their mate'. The definition of a 'mate' was broad, taking in anyone who was not in a position of authority. It is reasonable to think this arrangement emerged from the 'convict versus gaoler' social structure of the first white settlers. Convicts faced grave punishment if they were found to have reoffended, so it would have made sense to develop an informal regime of collective solidarity to protect one and all from prison, the lash or the gallows. Even rational ideas can be corrupted, though, and in time the original justification for not dobbing morphed into a simple 'just don't let on' attitude.

The conventions associated with dobbing are essentially to do with the virtue of loyalty. Loyalty requires that there be a deserving object—someone who has a legitimate claim on our allegiance. Such a claim might be based on family ties, citizenship or some other common bond. Traditionally even a monarch could forfeit that bond of loyalty, most often by oppressing their own people. More generally, however, loyalty is not owed to those who harm you or your interests.

Most people would agree that they owe no loyalty to a person who steals from them. A workplace thief might not do that directly, but if they go undetected they affect their colleagues as surely as they affect the organisation they work for. People who steal from their workplace or who are otherwise destructive of the common good do not deserve their colleagues' loyalty.

The first thing to note, then, is that we do not owe unqualified loyalty to our colleagues, although knowing this does not make it any easier if wrongdoing comes to our attention. For example, you might question the justice of the way your organisation is likely to respond. You might know that the person who has done the wrong thing is remorseful or that necessity forced them to do it. You might think any likely penalty would have a disproportionately negative effect on their life. You might even fear for your own wellbeing, not wanting to be drawn into an ugly situation with unpredictable consequences.

In view of those considerations, it could be tempting to do nothing. But to turn a blind eye is to become complicit in the wrongdoing. One option—a difficult one—is to confront the person you suspect of doing the wrong thing. They might provide additional information that explains their conduct; for example, a person who is not pulling their weight might reveal that they have recently been diagnosed with, say, a debilitating disease. That could explain everything.

Alternatively, confronting the person and seeing their reaction might confirm your suspicions. Instead of doing nothing more, you might offer them the opportunity to come forward voluntarily, to express remorse, and to seek to make good the deficiency. In most cases a voluntary admission of wrongdoing and a proposal for resti-tution will be well received. It might even be that your interven-tion constitutes the 'warning shot' the person has been waiting for. Chastened, they might adopt a completely new approach to work.

Finally, you might prefer to make a report—seeking protection under the relevant whistleblower policy. This can be an especially important step if the person you suspect of doing wrong is more senior. Having made a report, your task is done. It then falls to management to investigate, ensuring fairness for the accused person while protecting the interests of the organisation and its stakeholders.

THE QUESTIONS

Under what circumstances is it reasonable to report a colleague's poor performance or perceived wrongdoing?

In particular:

× Are you reasonably sure of your facts?

× Have you considered alternative explanations for the course of action you perceive as wrongdoing?

× Is it safe or proper to alert the person to your concerns or suspicions? Or is the matter so serious as to require immediate reporting to an authority—especially if there is a risk to health and safety?

× Is the suspected wrongdoer deserving of loyalty, or are they exploiting this virtue for their own advantage?

× Can your employer be relied on to make a fair and proportional response to what you might report?

× Are you exceeding the span of your authority? Are there other people who are aware of the situation and are better placed to act?

× Have you considered the potential consequences of taking action?

CRYING

After the death of my mother, many years passed before I was able to cry—not just in public but even in private. I had been seven years old at the time of our loss and, as the eldest of the children, I believed that I needed to be 'strong' for the sake of my siblings. No one told me that I should be like this. Perhaps I absorbed from my family environment, or from the prevailing culture, the idea that 'men don't cry'. For whatever reason, the grief was 'bottled' and the tears never came.

I suspect there are many other men of my age—and perhaps younger—who have internalised the same idea, that men should not grieve too openly and that 'tears are for women'. Such beliefs do neither gender good service. Apart from anything else, how we grieve seems to be more a matter of culture than biology. We thus have the ability to choose the modes by which grief is expressed. For example, some cultures have established rituals for grieving. These rituals set the patterns for how various members of the community should behave. In some cases, grief can be obvious (even extravagant) and include wailing, self-harm and prostration. Other cultures support a more subdued and private kind of grief.

Of course, not all crying need be associated with grief. We can cry in response to pain, in great mirth, in frustration, and in sympathy with others—as we might do when watching a film. Again, the context and cause of the tears seem to matter. For example, I have never heard of a person being embarrassed by the fact that they laughed until they cried.

This leads me to think that taboos against crying exist in circumstances where tears are seen as symbols of strength or weakness—probably further linked to the ability to exercise self-control.

THE QUESTIONS

Are there times when self-control might be inappropriate? For example, in what circumstances should we allow people to see that we share their grief or that we participate in a common experience of, say, vulnerability?

In particular:

- Have we taken account of the cultural context in which the expression of emotion is to occur?

- Are we influenced by gender stereotypes? If so, should they be challenged?

- Should we be careful to grieve in a manner that does not cause distress or annoyance to others? Or should they adjust to our needs at a difficult time?

DANGEROUS CREATURES

Human beings share the world with a marvellously diverse range of other creatures. Many are easy companions that either add to our lives or pass by largely unnoticed. There are, however, some that pose danger—when even the most casual encounter can involve mortal danger.

Humans have developed many ways of managing the risks; many of these involve capturing, maiming or killing the creatures posing the threat. In Australia, for example, after a number of people were bitten by sharks (some suffering fatal injuries), some state governments re-installed shark nets. While these nets are intended to separate the sharks from the people, they often lead to the deaths of marine animals (including sharks) that depend for their lives on free movement within the earth's oceans. Other interventions are the use of poisons to kill spiders and the capture and relocation of deadly snakes, crocodiles, and other creatures.

Apart from in works of fiction, sharks, spiders, crocodiles, and so on do not set out to harm humans. Instead, when we stray into their world, they respond opportunistically—either out of fear or instinctively, in the hope that we might prove to be a 'tasty morsel'. The problem is that in our attempts to preserve human life we might be punishing other creatures for doing nothing more than acting according to their nature.

Humans generally have a choice about whether or not to enter the environment of other creatures. Except in the case of accident, nothing compels us to challenge other top predators—such as crocodiles—in their own environment. We should also note that in some cultures the separation between humans and other creatures is not clear—with humans sharing kinship ties with other forms of life, including creatures that are rightly judged to be dangerous.

THE QUESTIONS

Given that humans are the ones endowed with the capacity to make choices, why should other creatures pay the ultimate price for our enjoyment of leisure (for example, so that we might spend a day at the beach) in safety? Does placing a high value on human life justify placing a relatively low value on the lives of other creatures, such that they can be killed whenever they threaten or inconvenience us?

In particular:

- Should humans take primary responsibility for avoiding contact with dangerous creatures, especially when entering their natural environment?

- Should we ensure that human lives are protected by means that cause the smallest possible amount of harm to other creatures — for example, by capturing and releasing spiders, rather than squishing them?

- If the natural world operates according to the principle of the survival of the fittest, should other creatures be expected to keep out of our way or accept the consequences?

DIFFICULT RELATIVES

Each year I hear stories of people anxiously preparing for family gatherings, often associated with a religious or cultural festival. There is a common pattern to their stories — relatives who are obnoxious, relatives who overstep the mark and try to discipline others' children, relatives spoiling for a fight over an ancient grievance that everyone else has let go but that defines their sense of identity. Alcohol can add fuel to the embers of family resentments and tensions, but even the most sober can self-combust in the hothouse of a family gathering. In some cases, the pressure to consume at a particular time and in a particular way is awful. Just one spark can ignite a fireball that scorches at least a few people who are otherwise enjoying their favourite festive fare. For the most part, though, people with 'difficult' relatives grit their teeth, smile, hug and hope for the best.

Of course, there are also families for whom seeing relatives is a delight and who come together with effortless pleasure. They might be the lucky few because, as the saying goes, we don't get to choose our relatives (or their spouses and children) — only our friends.

So what should we do when a relative behaves odiously? Should we make special allowances for them for the sake of blood or family harmony or should we call them to account?

THE QUESTIONS

Families, however they might be constituted, are an essential institution in all societies. Yet they are often made up of individuals you might never choose to associate with if given a choice. How do we manage difficult relatives while being true to our own values and principles?

In particular:

× Do you and your immediate family derive advantage from being part of your larger, extended family?

× Is your relative's behaviour merely annoying or does it violate your central values and principles?

× Is it possible to manage your relative's behaviour without causing a scene? For example, can the person be placed in the company of a family 'peace maker' who can prevent or limit the potential damage?

× Is your relative even aware of the effect he or she is having on others?

× Is your relative's behaviour harming others who cannot defend themselves?

- Will intervention be futile? Is the person unable or unwilling to change?

- If the person is the spouse of one of your blood relatives, would your blood relative be offended if you called either of them to account?

DISPOSING OF SURPLUS GADGETS

Until quite recently our local council used to collect e-waste (things such as old phones and computers) as part of household rubbish, but now the e-waste is excluded. So our small pile of old gadgets is beginning to grow. At some stage I will take the waste to a collection point, but for now it sits there gathering dust. This is despite the fact that it would be easy to slip the odd obsolete or broken phone into the food waste and send it off to landfill. Nobody would notice one old phone in the vast expanse of waste, and I would be free of a minor irritation.

THE QUESTIONS

Why should we act responsibly when it would be more convenient to pursue the selfish option – with little risk of being exposed?

Given that there is considerable value in an old phone—gold, rare earths, embedded energy, and so on, that could be recycled and put to further use—are we obliged to ensure that these resources are not squandered? One person's waste is another person's opportunity.

In particular:

- The earth has finite resources: wouldn't it be better to make do with less?

- × Someone will have to pay the price for the lost opportunity or the cost of preventable pollution. What if it is one of your children who ends up paying that price?

- × Is the burden of recycling really so hard to shoulder?

- × Are there ways to share the responsibility—for example, a community or street collection that you and your neighbours arrange?

DNA TESTING OF EMBRYOS

Some people are born with slim, athletic bodies, keen of eye and fleet of foot. Then there are people like me! Much of the joy in the world is to be found in its diversity, in the myriad sizes, shapes, skills and dispositions of humankind. The value of diversity is further reinforced by what is probably the most important ethical principle of all, what is known as 'respect for persons'. This principle recognises the fundamental dignity of every person, no matter what their gender, age, culture, sexual orientation, physical or mental abilities. Even a person who has committed the most awful of crimes is recognised as deserving of this degree of fundamental respect.

We say this respect is 'intrinsic', meaning that respect for persons cannot be earned and cannot be lost. It is simply something you deserve for being what you are—a person, a being capable of bearing the full range of rights and responsibilities. Human beings enjoy this status, regardless of their specific attributes, as a result of their partic-ipation, perhaps imperfectly, in a particular form of being—human being. This is why societies have increasingly come to acknowledge the intrinsic worth of people with different levels of ability, no matter whether those differences are an accident of birth, injury or disease.

We also know, however, that some humans are born into circumstances in which they are destined to suffer, not through any fault of their own but because of an unlucky roll of the genetic dice. These people deserve to be respected and cared for. But advances in science mean we can now test and analyse embryos to determine their genetic health, so it is possible to select embryos that will eventually grow into people who do not suffer from what have become avoidable conditions.

The question then becomes, 'Should we conduct these screening tests?' Should we select embryos to allow for 'family balancing' — choosing a female to add to an otherwise all-male set of children? Should we allow a deaf couple to select for a child who will be born deaf, so that he or she can grow up within the parents' culture? Should we select an embryo so that the resulting child will be suitable for donating an organ to an already sick sibling? And if we do make such choices will this lead society to turn its back on respect for diversity, with all parents with the means to do so seeking to select the 'perfect' child? Where should we stop?

Some of these questions are relatively easy to answer. For example, the principle of respect for persons would never allow us to create or use a person merely as a means to an end. No human may be treated simply as a tool. That is why slavery is an abomination and why it would be wrong to select a child purely to satisfy the desire of its parents to use it as a tissue bank to help save the life of a sibling.

We might, however, have more sympathy for parents wishing to prevent a child suffering from an avoidable disease. The difficulty lies in working out what precisely 'suffering' and 'disease' mean. For example, is autism a disease? If so, the world might never know some of its great geniuses. Is my poor eyesight a disease? Would the world be better off for having someone with better eyesight but none of my particular experience? What of Down syndrome or cerebral palsy? Think of all the amazing people who might never have been.

Finally, there is the question of what to do with the rejected embryo. As noted in the entry on abortion, some people accord an embryo, from the earliest stage, the status of personhood. I think this is mistaken. At the earliest stage of development a fertilised egg might be a form of human life, but there is a period before which it is impossible to ascribe to it an identity. So, providing the choice is made in the pre-implantation stage, or before, say, fourteen days after conception, I don't see an overwhelming problem in discarding an unwanted embryo. Nature does it all the time.

THE QUESTIONS

The main question here concerns what counts as adequate justification for using DNA testing to select an embryo, especially since what you decide could affect society's attitude to other people by setting a precedent for selecting embryos based on parental preferences—unrelated to the interests of the prospective child.

In particular:

- Are you testing for a genuine illness that causes not just inconvenience but actual suffering?

- Will the as yet unborn child be the primary beneficiary of the choice you make? That is, are you making the choice for the sake of your child and not for yourself or some other person?

- Would the world really be a better place if nobody were born with the condition you want to prevent?

- How will you help manage the risk that people born with the condition you want to avoid might feel in some way devalued?

THE GOLDEN RULE

Do unto others as you would have them do unto you.

DRESS CODES

A young woman recently told me her employer had set a minimum heel height of 4 centimetres—for women only. I gather high heels can be very uncomfortable to wear. And I have never heard it claimed that they improve performance. So what's going on?

There have been times in history when fashion really mattered. For example, under what were known as sumptuary laws, designed to control excessive spending, some types of clothing were forbidden for certain classes of people. This was common in times past, in both the East and the West. If you wore the wrong kind of button, for instance, you could find yourself in trouble. At other times there were strict rules governing what men, women and children might wear. In ancient Rome only men who had reached the age of political maturity could wear a toga. More recently, it is predominantly women who wear skirts and dresses in Western society, while men tend to be in shorts or trousers.

Sumptuary laws no longer apply and, apart from the purpose of safety or out of respect for religious, cultural or official protocols, there are no longer any rigid guidelines for what men or women should wear in Western society. When I visited the new Parliament House in Canberra soon after it was opened, the minimum dress standard was specified as 'tee shirt and thongs'—a relaxed standard for a relaxed nation. It seems that dress codes are now mostly a matter of taste, adjusted according to the individual's personal sense of decorum.

It does seem strange, therefore, when it is specified that there is no entry without a tie or jacket, that women may not wear trousers, or that women must wear high heels. Is this tradition at work? Is it a reaching for respect? Will anything of substance change if a man is not wearing a tie or a woman wears flat shoes? Would it not be sufficient just to ask for clean and neat attire?

Finally, some dress codes are designed to titillate, to exploit sexuality. This can be subtle or it can be screamingly overt. Some people are perfectly happy to go along with the specified style; others feel uncomfortable and vulnerable, especially if they do not perceive themselves as ideal or the norm.

THE QUESTIONS

Should we dress for comfort and to express our personal sense of style? Or should we adjust to meet the demands or expectations of others?

In particular:

× Are there any legitimate reasons (for example, safety) for adjusting your choice of clothes?

× Are you being respectful to others? Are they being respectful to you?

× Are others' expectations reasonable or just a matter of prejudice?

× Will you feel comfortable—physically, socially and emotionally—wearing these clothes?

EMPLOYERS AND EMPLOYEES

Businesses have a number of competing duties—to their owners, investors, customers, suppliers, wider society, and so on. In general, these duties are discharged by employees. This is always the case where the employer is a corporation. Corporations are just legal fictions, meaning they are not 'real', and their goals can be realised only through the work of real people.

Owners and investors make financial resources available to businesses. Historically, those resources will lie idle unless employees contribute their labour, intellect and skills to the mix, adding 'transformative value'.

Although the progressive use of robots and expert systems may make employers less reliant on human employees, for the time being the pursuit of enlightened self-interest (alone) would suggest that employees' welfare should be a high priority.

Among the basic 'goods' that should be afforded employees are the following:

× fair pay

× a safe and healthy workplace

× access to the best tools available

× respect and recognition for work well done

× fair treatment

× clarity concerning the organisation's purpose, values and principles

× the opportunity to be engaged in meaningful work.

The difficulty is that, beyond a bare minimum of goods, the needs of employees vary considerably. For example, some employees need to operate within tight boundaries while others need freedom to innovate; some need to work limited hours while others want to expand and shrink their hours of work according to changing priorities; some want to be left alone to get on with their work while others want to be involved in every decision.

The answer to this variety lies with both employer and employee. Each employee has a responsibility to find a job that best fits their personal style and preferences. Employers need to be flexible to a degree, but they are entitled to establish the kind of culture that will best suit the purpose, values and principles of the enterprise. They must also provide the basic goods just listed, but beyond that it is up to employees to decide whether or not they are suited to the organisation. If not, they will usually have the option of trying to find a place that better accommodates their aspirations.

Of course, this can change as a result of technological innovation. Employees may have fewer choices if they wish to retain a job. Indeed, one of the most pressing challenges facing society as a whole concerns how best to respond to changes in the employment prospects of citizens.

THE QUESTIONS

For the time being, employees are vital to the success of an enterprise. What then might be an employer's primary obligations? Where does responsibility lie between employees and employers once the basic obligations have been met?

In particular:

- Are the basic 'goods', as outlined, being provided?

- Are employees truly free to find other employment if the culture of an organisation does not suit their personal preferences?

- Are employees in a position to freely express their misgivings, hopes, and so on?

- Do you assess the potential cultural fit—the alignment of purpose, values and principles—when selecting potential employees or choosing where to work?

ETHICAL PURCHASING

Every purchasing decision we make helps shape a market and, in turn, aspects of the world. We can base our decisions solely on factors such as price, practical utility and status, or we can adopt a broader set of criteria. The reality is that the market is indifferent to our reasons. From a market perspective it is no more rational to choose something because it is red than it is to choose something because it will help reduce global poverty. In that sense the market is amoral and pays no regard to ethics, reason or any notion of intrinsic value.

It is up to us to determine what is important. One thing to take into account is the conditions under which people produce the goods and services we consume. For the most part, we are ignorant of this; it usually takes a disaster of some kind or a campaign of exposure by the media or a non-government organisation to come face to face with those who form the supply chain. And the revelations can be shocking—people working in unsanitary places, paid a pittance, working cruelly long hours, with little hope of education or advancement. Stories and images can prick the conscience of consumers, with the result that some products are boycotted and others favoured.

Ethical consumption can be slightly more expensive at the start, and not everybody can afford the additional cost. But the more people favour an ethical market, the greater is its volume of sales and the lower the unit cost of production becomes. In the end, if everybody demands ethically produced goods and services the market will move to an affordable price point.

The trouble is it is not always easy to determine what is ethical in supply chains and production. For example, some producers use child labour in circumstances where the alternatives facing the children are far worse than working in a factory; similarly, some adults work in difficult and dangerous conditions, often separated from family and friends, but they do so because that is their 'least bad' option. The challenge is to distinguish between situations that are genuinely in transition—from bad to better to good—and those that are stuck with bad practices that you might inadvertently be supporting. Care needs to be taken to avoid so trenchant a position as to deny opportunities for improvement among those who are making a genuine effort, albeit from a low base. Instead, we should try to structure our purchasing in such a way as to ensure that nothing is obtained from the laggards who make no effort to improve.

Working out who to trust and who to buy from can be difficult because manufacturers and retailers know it is in their interests to appear to be ethical. There are, however, some clues an ethical consumer can be reasonably confident about. The Fairtrade movement and logo can be relied on, along with the marks of other non-profit certifiers who provide assurances that goods and services have been produced in accordance with proper standards for human rights, environmental sustainability, and so on.

Most importantly, look for certifiers that support high levels of transparency—that can show you evidence of progress for people and practices and that claim to be improving conditions, as opposed to having achieved perfection.

THE QUESTIONS

Our purchasing decisions make a difference. The more people support ethical buying the cheaper the products become. But how do we ensure that our good intentions don't end up producing bad outcomes, especially for the most vulnerable in this world?

In particular:

- Do you know about the conditions under which the things you are buying were produced? Can you find out?

- If children are involved in production, are their conditions improving over time? For example, is work combined with education?

- Would children involved in the production of goods or the provision of services be worse off if they were not working in these jobs—for example, would they otherwise be sold into prostitution?

- Do you pay attention to reliable guides to ethical procurement, such as the Fairtrade movement?

- Do you tell retailers you want to buy goods and services that have been ethically produced and obtained?

ETHICS AND THE SHOPPING TROLLEY

In a market economy one of the most powerful ways of shaping the world is through your purchasing decisions. It might seem that a single person cannot make much of a difference, but by the time every person's individual choices are aggregated the force for change can be irresistible. This is because businesses ultimately succeed or fail according to their capacity to provide goods and services that consumers value.

The customer is sovereign in the market. No person can tell you what is a good or bad basis for making a choice. Advertisers might try to persuade us of the superiority of the goods and services they promote, but in the end it is up to us to decide what matters most — price, a brand name, a colour, some ethical impact in the world, for example.

The main thing with shopping is to try to avoid falling into habits that make you blind to the effect of the choices you make. It is easy to pick up a familiar brand without thinking about its actual properties. Every time we do this there is a risk that we inadvertently cause something to happen in the world that we would never condone. It might be an employee being exploited or an animal being treated cruelly, or it might be degradation of the natural environment or even a risk to health through the spread of unsafe or unhealthy products.

Information about the things we are buying is becoming easier to find as a result of using online resources or of legislation dealing with product labelling. It is becoming less difficult to ascertain where things are made, what they contain, and what some of their larger impacts in the world might be.

Not every person has the money required to make perfect choices, but all of us have the capacity to link the contents of our shopping trolley to our central values and principles and then do the best we can with what we have.

THE QUESTIONS

Our shopping choices matter. They can force businesses to improve their practices and limit the harm they do in the world. Markets allow for our individual choices to be amplified. In view of this, how do we make the best choices possible?

In particular:

- Do you know what really matters to you and the people you care about? That is, are your central values and principles clear?

- When you come across advertising do you decode the messages the businesses are trying to send? Are those messages consistent with the kind of person you want to be?

- Do you know the impact of the choices you currently make? Are you in a position to insist on more information to help you make informed decisions?

- Might technology be enlisted to help—perhaps product barcodes that take you to reliable sources of information?

- Do you look for certification marks that you can trust—for example, Fairtrade and RSPCA?

- Is price your principal basis for selecting products? If so, is this a matter of choice or necessity? Could your choices help to lower the price of goods you prefer?

EUTHANASIA AND SUICIDE

The right to life is fundamental but not absolute; that is, there are circumstances when that right can be forfeited—for example, if you threaten the life of another person who in turn uses force to resist your attack, even to the point that it leads to your death. Beyond rare exceptions of this kind, though, the right to life is considered inviolable.

Opinions differ when it comes to how the right to life arises. Some religions teach that life is the gift of god (or the gods); other belief systems see life as having intrinsic value, no matter where it comes from. So, instead of seeing life as a gift (that can be given and taken away), the alternative is to see life as belonging to the individual who is alive. These different outlooks tend to shape the debate about euthanasia and physician-assisted suicide.

Most cultures have established laws against homicide. As a result, people who deliberately kill other human beings are usually at risk of suffering the most severe of penalties—including, in some societies, death. It is worth noting here that the thing that makes murder wrong is not that you will be punished for this wrongdoing: the 'wrongness' lies in the violation of the moral right to life. The punishment for proven guilt is a predictable adverse consequence, but the fault is intrinsic to the act. It should also be noted that some groups of people—notably healers such as medical professionals—have traditionally been expected to work to preserve life. There has often been public alarm at the idea that a doctor might kill one of his or her own patients.

Suicide is a different matter. In some societies it was widely accepted that suicide was a reasonable (and sometimes necessary) practice. The ancient Romans, for example, saw no shame in suicide; if anything, the act of killing oneself was considered honourable. This accorded with ancient Romans' dominant view that one's life was one's own to live and to end. Later, however, under the influence of Christianity, human life was redefined as being the gift of God. Indeed, the doctrine eventually developed into a belief that a person did not even own their own body (or any part of it), a position still reflected in the law. Wherever Christian (or similar) religious views are dominant, suicide is outlawed. A person who commits the 'mortal sin' of killing themselves is believed to be condemned to an eternity of suffering in Hell and their mortal remains may not be buried in hallowed ground, which is reserved for those who have died from other causes. In view of the dominance of Christianity in shaping Western civilisation, it is not surprising that suicide has for so long been considered not only tragic but also shameful.

Suicide committed by people who are suffering from mental illness and who would otherwise prefer life is indeed tragic. So is suicide committed by people who feel trapped by their circumstances and would choose to go on living if there were any other possibility of escaping their predicament. But there is a third class of people for whom death is a rational choice they might take up freely and in good conscience.

We all know that human suffering can be terrible. In some cases it cannot be assuaged by anything short of the sufferer's death. It is a simple fact that not all forms of pain can be relieved by the medical arts and sciences.

Imagine the following scenario—not at all far-fetched. From time to time there are accidents in which people are trapped in, say, burning vehicles or buildings. One hopes they will lose consciousness before enduring the agony of being burnt alive. But we cannot be sure that will happen. Suppose you came across such a scene—a vehicle on fire, no hope of putting out the flames, no way to rescue the trapped person. And suppose you have the means to kill the person quickly and surely (perhaps you are a police officer, armed with a pistol). What would you do? What *should* you do?

I once asked a Catholic priest what he would do in a situation such as this. He had no hesitation in saying he would end the life of the sufferer, as quickly and humanely as possible. He doubted that his God would disapprove of an act done out of love and compassion for the suffering person. In other words, he doubted that what he proposed to do would be sinful and, if it was, he counted on his God being merciful.

If your instinct would be to end the life of the sufferer, you will understand the case of those who argue in favour of euthanasia (where you play an active role in ending the life of the sufferer) or assisted suicide (where you help a person to kill themselves).

Of course, any society that legalises either euthanasia or assisted suicide needs to face up to the reality of what it is allowing—the deliberate killing of one human being by another. Further, if medical professionals are to be involved, which they should be, we would be fundamentally altering the ethos of a profession that has been dedicated to healing and the preservation of human life.

Many doctors have resolved this dilemma by applying what is known as the 'principle of double effect', which allows for the possi-bility of negative double effects (such as the death of a patient) just so long as the death is not intended and the means used for the primary purpose (usually pain relief) are not illicit. So, for example, it has been common practice for doctors to prescribe increasing doses of opiates such as morphine, knowing that this will eventually cause a patient to die from respiratory failure. The doctors who do this do not intend to kill the patient: they simply want to ease the pain, although they expect that death will be the unintended consequence of their treatment.

Some will ask why we need to consider euthanasia or assisted suicide if this kind of ultimate relief is already available? The answer is that many people who are suffering want to die with dignity: they do not want to slip into a drug-induced coma before drifting away. More importantly, they want to be in control of their own death—and not have such a vitally important, personal decision resting in the hands of a physician they might scarcely know. In many cases their aim is to 'make peace with the world', to say farewell to loved ones, and to depart this life on their own terms.

Central to this is the requirement that people seeking to end their suffering be in a position to make their choice freely. In contrast, one of the concerns expressed by critics of euthanasia and assisted suicide is that vulnerable people will be forced or induced into ending their life for the convenience of others. Various proposals have been put forward—and in the case of the Netherlands enshrined in law—to prevent this kind of exploitation or mistake. The evidence to date is that such measures are effective and that free, prior and informed consent can be assured. It has also become clear that people facing unendurable suffering often obtain the wherewithal to end their lives and then, comforted by the knowledge that they have what is needed, live on without exercising their right to die. Just knowing that they can end their life, in dignity and at a time of their choosing, is sufficient.

THE QUESTIONS

Since neither euthanasia nor assisted suicide is lawful in Australia at present, would you urge a change in legislation? If that is not possible, are there circumstances in which you would risk prosecution in order to help another person die?

In particular:

- Does your ethical framework—including your religious and cultural beliefs—treat human life as a personal right or as a gift to be preserved at the pleasure of another (such as god)?

- Is the suffering you encounter truly unable to be relieved by any means other than the death of the sufferer?

- Is the sufferer genuinely able to give free, prior and informed consent to the ending of their life?

- Are the means available to ensure a dignified death?

- Is anyone encouraging the person's death likely to gain from the death—inherit money, be relieved of a debt, escape the obligations of a carer, and so on? If so, is this warping the decision-making process?

- Are disinterested professional advisers—doctors and counsellors, for example—involved?

- Does the person who is suffering truly have control over the decision-making process relating to their dying, including multiple opportunities to change their mind, even right until the end?

- If you are to be involved, are you prepared to be fully accountable for your actions, including coping with the potential legal consequences? If so, what is it about your relationship with the sufferer that makes you prepared to take on this obligation? What are your real motivations?

FAMILY TYPES

History suggests that people label as normal whatever family structure exists in their time and place. For example, many cultures think of the extended family as the norm. Members of extended families typically live in close proximity, the various generations sharing duties in such areas as child-rearing, economic production, and ritual and religious duties.

In modern Western societies, however, the extended family has given way to the nuclear family: a couple of parents and their children living relatively self-contained lives has become the new normal. Yet what is normal varies considerably. For example, the death and internment of so many young men during World Wars 1 and 2 meant that it became necessary for society to accept as normal a single mother raising her children alone. These single mothers no longer attracted frowns; people no longer automatically thought these children would be irredeemably harmed by the absence of a father in their home. And in fact there are now many families that do not contain children, be that a matter of choice or of necessity.

THE QUESTIONS

Apart from familiarity with your own family structure, are there good reasons for approving or disapproving of any other type of family structure?

In particular:

× Are there religious or cultural factors that will affect family members' ability to integrate with their community?

× Are traditions suitable for an earlier time and another culture placing a 'dead hand' on new ways of establishing a stable and happy environment for family life?

× Is a proposed family structure sufficiently flexible and functional to allow family members the freedom to flourish on their own terms? For example, does the family structure allow for individual differences and the accommodation of reasonable personal preferences?

× Is a proposed family structure fair, or does it merely replicate historic forms of injustice—for example, placing an inequitable burden on women?

× Does the family's life privilege or disadvantage one generation compared with another?

FREE FOOD

One of the most important and interesting characteristics of human beings is the fact that we regularly choose to do what we think is good or right, even when there is no external compulsion to do so. More remarkable still is the fact that we frequently make such choices, even if it means not getting something we want. People tend to look for grand instances of this, but simple cases abound. Many workplaces, for example, display boxes of sweets or other goods that are freely available and for which a donation is expected. Nobody monitors these goods, and it would be easy to take an item without making a contribution. Yet people regularly do the right thing even though the risk of being caught behaving badly is negligible.

Perhaps the main variable here is the value of what is at stake. When what is at stake is trivial—access to a chocolate, say—why risk undermining one's own ethical foundations, why risk damage to one's own character? But suppose that something more important is at stake. If your children were starving, would you steal food for them? And if you could do that without detection, what then?

British philosopher John Locke argued that we cannot claim as our own property anything more than we can use without being wasteful. Thus, if a farmer has an orchard in which apples lie uncollected you are free to take the surplus, no matter whether fences have been built or warnings given.[13] Most goods, however, are not left lying about at risk of perishing: instead, they are preserved or converted into a stable store of value (such as money). Additionally, if you believe in good conscience that it is essential, for the good of others, for you to engage in dishonesty, are you prepared to accept the consequences? To accept the consequences would be a mark of your sincerity and would distinguish you from the common criminal.

Where possible, affluent societies make available basic welfare products so that no person is forced by necessity to act unethically or unlawfully. Yet people can still fall through the cracks in the system.

Then there are those who live outside the system altogether, who do not recognise the legitimacy of society's rules and act solely for the sake of self, family or some other defined or undefined reason. These are society's criminals—individuals who operate outside the law. They are not driven so much by necessity as by a desire to prey

---

13 See Locke, J (2010,) *Second Treatise of Government*, section 36, http://www.gutenberg.org/files/7370/7370-h/7370-h.htm.

on others. They are sometimes bound by their own ethical code, but this typically applies to only a limited set of people and, in any case, it fails to protect wider society from predation. For such people the risk of being caught is the primary deterrent.

THE QUESTIONS

Most people are honest, even when there is no obvious advantage in being so. Are there circumstances in which dishonesty should be excused?

In particular:

× Is what you propose to do consistent with the kind of character you hope to develop?

× Is the person trusting in your honesty doing so in good faith and for good reason?

× Do you depend on the honesty of others? Is there a reciprocal obligation?

× Are your circumstances so desperate as to lead you to consider taking something that is not yours? Are your unmet needs truly essential, rather than just a matter of convenience?

× Is there any alternative way to meet your essential needs—anything at all (even if it brings personal cost) that would allow you to avoid the taint of dishonesty?

× Is the object you might take going to waste in any case?

× Are you willing to pay the penalty if called to account for your decisions?

FREEDOM OF INFORMATION

In a democracy the power a government exercises ultimately derives from the citizens in whose name the government acts. The government's authority is renewed or withdrawn from time to time by way of elections, when citizens are entitled to make a choice about the performance of their representatives in parliament and of the government that has exercised executive power since the preceding election.

A democratic government is therefore crucially dependent on its citizens having access to information on which to base their decisions. This principle has led to the creation of 'freedom of information' schemes, which are notionally designed to make available to citizens information about the operations of government ministers and public servants. I say 'notionally' because such schemes are usually designed to hide as much as to disclose, using administrative red tape, costs and exceptions to maintain as much government secrecy as possible.

The media have traditionally played an important role in finding, verifying and analysing government information for the benefit of citizens. In the so-called information age, however, the release of government information has also occurred by other means—for example, by the Julian Assange–founded organisation WikiLeaks.

Governments strenuously object to the operations of organisations such as WikiLeaks. They tolerate freedom of information schemes and have learnt to live with the scope and scale of most media investigations, but they see organisations and individuals that make available and publish vast quantities of leaked material as far greater sources of risk. Their objections to the leaking of material vary in strength and nature. The strongest objections usually relate to perceived threats to national security—especially to the lives and welfare of covert operatives who might be exposed. An associated concern is that strategic rivals will benefit from access to information that would otherwise have been kept secret.

Governments also object to a break in the 'orderly management' of affairs. They argue that their well-designed and proper processes are undermined by leaks and that they need to be able to test ideas and seek advice in confidence. This, they say, is the basis for the development of sound public policy. In the absence of confidentiality, people will not be open about what they really think and avoidable mistakes will be made.

This last point extends beyond the domestic to international considerations. For example, WikiLeaks published a vast trove of diplomatic cables that exposed the inner thoughts of government officials. Full transparency undoubtedly caused embarrassment to various governments, and it was argued that diplomats will make candid assessments only if they know that they can do so in confidence.

Those supporting WikiLeaks make a number of points in response to these objections. First, they say they are careful to ensure that nothing that could expose an individual to risk is revealed. Second, they say government secrecy can be used for good or for ill and they seek only to expose wrongdoing—as in the case of Bradley (now Chelsea) Manning, in which the US government was revealed to be spying on its own citizens at home. Third, they claim it is hypocritical for governments to complain about people obtaining and using secret information: government intelligence services do it all the time. Finally, they argue that the risk of embarrassment is a small price for governments to bear when compared with the value of a well-informed citizenry.

There is, presumably, a balance to be found between these two stances. It is obviously wrong to use secrecy provisions to cover up illegal or unethical conduct on the part of governments. Equally, there are some things that ought to be secret, and the mere fact that a person wants to know something does not mean they have a right to that knowledge. For example, in a time of war it is perfectly acceptable to keep secrets from your enemy—and to mislead them where possible. The challenge is to ensure that secrecy provisions are not used simply for the convenience of a government but are used solely in the national interest.

Finally, there is a fundamental question to do with when, or whether, it is acceptable to break the law. The leaking of confidential government information is usually deemed illegal, and citizens have a prima facie, or fundamental, obligation to obey the law. Some people are bound by specific obligations, such as oaths or promises, that, if broken, attract high penalties. Yet there are some individuals who have deliberately chosen to break the law—including in relation to secrecy.

From an ethical, as opposed to legal, perspective, it might be permissible, even required, for a citizen to break what they in good conscience see to be an unjust law. For example, in Australia there used to be laws that made it an offence for a 'white man' to live with an Aboriginal woman. This was undoubtedly an unjust law, and any person would have been within their rights to disregard it out of affection for a loved one, whatever their ethnicity. Similarly, during the Vietnam War some young men refused to serve in the military, even though they were conscripted to do so; these men were standing true to their principles as conscientious objectors.

A fundamental test of the sincerity of a conscientious objector lies in whether or not the person is willing to face the consequences of their decision to disobey the law as a matter of principle. In some cases, to wait to face the consequences would be futile since the consequences could also be unjust. A well-ordered society would acknowledge this and allow for the possibility of conscientious objection by imposing moderate penalties in cases where illegal conduct is entirely motivated by principle and a concern for the public good. This, of course, would not extend to acts of treason, when the conduct is intended to harm the nation.

THE QUESTIONS

In what circumstances is it reasonable (and responsible) to make available for publication material that a government claims to be secret or confidential?

In particular:

- Are the secrecy provisions being used to hide wrongdoing?

- Will publication of the information put innocent people at risk?

- Will publication of the information damage the national interest—as opposed to the interests of the government of the day?

- Would the information being revealed genuinely help citizens to make better informed decisions?

- Are you bound by an overriding pledge or commitment to maintain confidentiality?

- Is what you propose to do illegal?

- Are you willing to accept the costs of your actions?

FREEDOM OF SPEECH

A vibrant society is marked by its promotion and preservation of a number of basic liberties. In a liberal democracy, in particular, one of the most important of these is freedom of speech. Some people argue that this right should be unfettered and that even the most objectionable comments should be brought out in the open. Part of this argument is that the sunlight of public exposure will weaken the hold of ideas that could flourish and multiply in the dark.

Others think there should be some limits to freedom of speech. For example, it is claimed that there is an important distinction between 'liberty', which should be taken with responsibility, and 'licence', which is unconstrained. The case often used to argue for some limitation concerns a person who maliciously calls out 'Fire!' in a crowded theatre, causing people to panic. The objection to this is based on the classic liberal position of English philosopher John Stuart Mill: 'The only purpose for which power can be rightfully exercised over any member of a civilized community, against his will, is to prevent harm to others.'[14]

Mill's approach is not just designed to constrain the power of the state: it is also meant to apply to person-to-person relations. Indeed, it is designed to enlarge to the greatest extent possible the liberty of the individual. If any action is not harmful to others (whether or not formally proscribed) we ought to be free to do as we like. This would therefore rule out defamation and other wrongs, even if a person might be able to sue for redress in the courts.

The idea of harm caused by words is not an abstract concept. There are Australians alive today who experienced some of the worst horrors of the twentieth century under Adolf Hitler's Nazi

---

14 Mill, JS (1975), 'On liberty', *Three Essays*, OUP, Oxford, UK.

Germany. The shadow of those events looms over the discussion of free speech. Some think it fanciful to suggest that such things could happen in Australia. It is worth noting, though, that enlightened German opinion would have been the same before the ascent of the Nazis, who devoted much of their political rhetoric to the task of dehumanising the Jews of Europe. Using both imagery and words, Nazi propaganda sought to portray the Jewish people as not fully human—even comparing them with vermin in the most specific terms.

A liberal democracy should uphold a presumptive right to free speech. This right should, however, be rebuttable in limited circumstances where the law expressly prohibits specific forms of expression, as might apply in cases of national security, child pornography, and so on. If we are to avoid the worst of what happened in the past, though, it could be argued that we should go further and protect people from two forms of speech:

- stating or implying that another person is undeserving of the fundamental respect owed each human being regardless of race, religion, gender, age, sexual orientation, or other such characteristics

- inciting violence against or hatred of another person because of their race, religion, gender, age, sexual orientation or other such characteristics.

Importantly, such an approach would not protect people from lesser forms of insult or offence, no matter how unpleasant they might be for the person insulted or offended. If someone wants to insult or offend me, that might be the cost of liberty for all—just as long as they do not cross the lines just proposed.

One might hope that such laws would be unnecessary and that a maximum degree of freedom would be accompanied by an equivalent measure of ethical restraint. But history shows that the risks of relying on such informal measures are too great.

THE QUESTIONS

A society is better off for having the greatest possible degree of free speech, yet the harm caused by words is not necessarily abstract or minor. How then do we strike a balance?

In particular:

x Is what you are about to say going to cause harm to others? If so, would you be better keeping quiet?

x Are you directly or indirectly calling into question the humanity of another person?

x You might be hurt or offended, but have you actually been harmed?

x Is the thing you find offensive best kept out in the open?

x Is the language used merely 'robust'? Is this one of the costs of democracy?

x Do you have an equal right of reply? Do others have the same opportunity to have their voices heard?

FUTURE GENERATIONS: OUR OBLIGATION

Many cultures honour their ancestors, allowing their memory to shape current practices—visiting shrines, saying prayers for the dead, and so on—yet the same attention is rarely, if ever, paid to generations yet to come. This is despite the fact that our children and their children will ultimately have to cope with the legacy we leave. Should we do more to honour our obligation to secure their future?

Part of the answer to this question relates to the way we think about the concepts of time and progress. For much of human history time was thought of in terms of circles, or cycles. The cyclical nature of the seasons, decay and renewal, night and day led people to believe that the future would be much like the past. The idea of progress is a marker of modernity, a product of the optimistic belief that human ingenuity will lead to improvements in the world. Despite wars and disasters caused by human mismanagement, that general hope has remained alive—until now.

It now seems possible that our descendants will inherit a future that is worse than our present. Global warming, terrorism, geopolitical instability, stagnant and deflating economies, water wars, technical disruption—these and other factors loom large as potential sources of risk. The good news is that it is not inevitable that the bleakest of outlooks will become a reality. Instead of just assuming that the future will be better than the past, however, we need to take steps to ensure this. We have a choice.

One of the philosophical tools we can use to help guide us is to look through what philosopher John Rawls refers to as a 'veil of ignorance'.[15] In thinking about how we might make decisions that accord with justice, Rawls proposes that we look to a future in which

---

15 Rawls, J (1999), A *Theory of Justice*, HUP, Boston.

we do not know where we will be born and in what condition. We might be the poorest of the poor; we might be born with a terrible disease; we might be born into wealth and power. The main thing is that we do not know where we will land, and Rawls suggests that this not knowing will lead us to make decisions that will not disadvantage future generations.

It might seem impossible to imagine in detail every person's circumstances. An alternative approach is to focus on the global commons[16] — those things, such as the environment and international security, on which all people depend. This might help to focus our attention on ensuring that the common goods we inherited from our predecessors are preserved or enhanced for our descendants.

Our descendants cannot speak for themselves, but we can imagine what they might say and do, especially how they might judge us if we rob them of a future of the quality we have claimed for ourselves. In the absence of any penalty we might have to pay, conscience alone can guide us.

THE QUESTIONS

We will never meet most of our descendants, and they have no capacity to hold us to account. So why should we worry about their interests? Why not make the most of the world we live in and let posterity look after itself?

In particular:

× Are you at all concerned about the judgment of history?

---

16 Jacobs, M (2016), 'Are we failing future generations?', The Ethics Centre, Sydney, http://www.ethics.org.au/on-ethics/blog/august-2016/are-we-failing-our-duties-to-future-generations.

- How would you like to find things if you were born, say, a hundred years from now?

- If you are not concerned for all future people, what about those who are your direct descendants?

- Have you imagined, or can you imagine, what life might be like in a world where the global commons has been degraded?

- How might your everyday decisions—in relation to energy use, purchasing, investments, and so on—be shaping the world of the future? Are you making matters better or worse for your children and grandchildren?

- What are the most important things you can influence today for the future?

- If there is an obligation to the future, does it fall only on the affluent? Or is it a matter for everyone who is alive today?

- Should individual liberty be constrained in the interests of the as yet unborn?

GAMBLING

If you strip the phenomenon of gambling back to its essence—that is, the taking of calculated risks in the hope of reward—it turns out to be a relatively benign pastime. In fact, we gamble all the time, crossing the road without using a pedestrian crossing, investing in the stock market, trying a new and untested product, and so on.

The evils associated with gambling are actually external to the pastime. People are right to be concerned about addiction to gambling and the involvement of organised crime, but addiction to anything (drugs, work, sex, whatever) is a problem, as is organised crime. As a result, unless you oppose risk-taking in general, or disapprove of enrichment by means that do not require personal effort, it is not gambling itself that raises ethical questions.

For their part, gambling businesses argue that they are offering an entertainment service, one for which they charge a fee (their margin of wins over losses) in return for giving the 'punters' the thrill of a bet and the possibility of a win. Unfortunately, however, some gambling enterprises seek to exploit external evils such as addiction for their own advantage. Rather than removing aspects of gaming that might 'hook' someone, they frequently turn up the dial, looking for ways to increase a person's dependence on the game and thus increase their frequency of use. A range of skills are harnessed to achieve this result, among them those of designers and psychologists.

Additionally, even if gambling were to remain entirely innocent as a pastime, you can still have too much of a good thing. Choirs singing popular songs might be a pleasant enough diversion, but this does not mean we should hope to find one on every corner. Yet gambling is becoming ubiquitous, creeping into every corner of our lives in real time and increasingly online. Some parents now say their children know more about the odds at a footy match than they do about the players, with the effect that a family outing that used to be enjoyed for the sake of the time spent together and the sporting prowess of the players is being reduced to a commercial platform for punters and the companies that seek to profit from them. And let there be no mistake: in the end 'the house' wins.

Finally, it seems that young men are especially susceptible to online betting and that, like other gamblers, they are not very good at monitoring and controlling their losses, meaning that other important uses of money (such as saving) are being neglected.

THE QUESTIONS

Gambling might be an innocent enough pastime in its purest and simplest form, but what happens when it is 'engineered' to be addictive or starts to occupy every aspect of our lives?

In particular:

- ✗ Are you hooked or at risk of being hooked on gambling? Are you really in control?

- ✗ Are you aware of the tricks that might be used to help empty your wallet? For example, does the gambling company make you feel important or as though it is one of your 'mates'?

- ✗ Are you really gambling with spare cash, or should you be spending this money on other things, especially when you have obligations to others—for rent, food, school fees, and so on?

- ✗ Is your fundamental experience being changed by gambling? Has what you once enjoyed about an activity been lost in favour of betting?

GENDER AND THE WORKPLACE

It remains a fact of Australian life that a woman doing the same job as a man is often paid less. The same evidence of bias can be seen in the relatively small proportion of women who fill the upper ranks of management and who sit on boards.

Such variations in remuneration and opportunity cannot be explained by intrinsic differences in skill: women are at least as well educated as men and perform just as well, so there is no obvious justification for the difference in their rewards. This leaves only two other possible explanations—first, that structural or cultural factors give rise to differences in lifelong productivity by men and women; second, that women are subject to discrimination.

It used to be the case that patterns of child-bearing and child-rearing were such that women needed to take extended periods of leave from the workplace. In their absence, men would advance to more senior positions, and the women would be left to take on more junior roles when they returned to work. Nowadays, the availability of child care, greater flexibility in working arrangements and changing patterns of parental care have reduced the differential in the amount of time spent at work by men and women.

Yet even if these factors hold good, they offer no explanation for the fact that women continue to be paid less than men doing the same job. All other things being equal, this can only be explained as a consequence of prejudice against women, which is unlikely to be restricted in its application to remuneration and is likely to apply in other areas, such as hiring and promotion.

A number of employers are now trying to eliminate gender as a factor when hiring people or assessing them for promotion. This involves removing from resumés any information that would allow the gender of the applicant to be known or inferred. Experiments have shown that the same resumé will be treated differently according to the perceived gender of the applicant, selection panels rationalising their choices by giving priority to whatever factors best supported their underlying preference. Such 'gender-blind' evaluations should help to minimise the effects attributable to bias, their aim being the making of judgments solely on the basis of merit and performance.

The relatively small proportion of women in senior executive ranks and boardrooms is sometimes explained by the claim that there are not enough qualified candidates to fill the roles. This is unconvincing—especially now that there is a growing number of programs designed to ensure a ready supply of women able to take on even the most demanding roles.

But why be concerned about this? The first reason is to do with justice. How can it be fair to treat people of equal merit and capacity in a discriminatory fashion? Second, how can society be well served by artificially limiting access to the talents of half the population? Third, there is considerable practical advantage in boosting diversity in the workplace: the last thing needed in a modern, innovative economy is a tendency towards 'group think'. Gender is not the only type of diversity that should be encouraged, but it is a good start.

Another point concerns customers' and investors' ability to help shape this agenda. Although business owners and managers quite properly claim a right to autonomy in how they operate, including in terms of appointments to boards and other positions, a similar degree of autonomy should be afforded customers and investors, who are free to take into account questions of equity when determining what to buy and where to invest. In this way self-interest and principle combine to support genuine equality of opportunity for men and women in the workplace.

Finally, it seems that when remuneration is determined by negotiation women routinely ask for less than men. They also tend to underestimate their capacity to do a job (believing they need to be a 'perfect fit'), whereas men tend to assume that near enough is good enough and therefore apply for positions that will stretch their capacity to perform. Greater availability of information about relative levels of pay might help solve the first problem: presumably women would ask for the same pay as men if they knew what the benchmark was. Perhaps the evidence of successful female role models will help redress the second problem. In both cases men can be helpful by encouraging women to set their sights at least as high as their male counterparts.

THE QUESTIONS

Is there any justification for men and women receiving differential rewards and opportunities in the workplace?

In particular:

× How would you feel if you received less pay than someone else for doing the same job to the same level of accomplishment?

× Have you actively sought out and encouraged female applicants with a capacity to do the job?

× Have you considered what other parties might think of a business that lacks gender balance or is inequitable in its treatment of men and women?

- × Are you making any unwarranted assumptions about the relative capacity of men and women to perform various tasks?

- × Have you structured your workplace so as to allow for flexibility of a kind that will facilitate equal opportunity for women and men?

- × Would you be proud to see full public disclosure of details of your employment practices?

GENETICALLY MODIFIED ORGANISMS

If you believe in evolution you believe in genetic modification. The process of natural selection rewards efficient and effective developments not only in the phenome of organisms (how they look on the outside) but also in their genome (the genetic instruction kit that is at work on the inside). The trouble with genetically modified organisms is that they are typically thought to be a product of unnatural selection, whereby humans are perceived to have interfered with the proper order of nature. In turn, this gives rise to a number of fears, the most prominent of which are the following:

- × the release of a dangerous organism that can be neither stopped nor contained as a consequence of its capacity for further evolution and self-replication

- × the degradation of naturally occurring substances and species, leaving nothing that is a pure product of nature

- × a fear that human ingenuity has exceeded the proper boundaries set by a divine overseer.

Agricultural chemical company Monsanto (in)famously failed to take such considerations into account when releasing some of the earliest commercial varieties of GMOs. Focusing its attention on farmers and making the case that GMOs would produce cheaper and more effective plant varieties, Monsanto paid little or no attention to the fact that consumers might choose not to buy GMOs for food. So it turned out, and farmers discovered that there was little point in growing food nobody wants to buy.

The bad experience with Monsanto has led people to pay far more attention to popular concerns about GMOs. Yet, despite scientists' and regulators' best efforts, people remain uneasy about developments that involve genes crossing the species barrier—for example, putting a gene from a fish into a tomato. It does not matter that the building blocks are the same at the molecular level: the 'unnatural' exchange still causes alarm.

The case for GMOs is generally best made when there are clear advantages arising from innovation and when human consumption is not involved. For example, there has been little criticism of programs designed to eliminate mosquito-borne diseases such as malaria and Zika virus by modifying the genes of mosquitoes. In such cases the advantages for human health and wellbeing seem obvious enough to warrant broad acceptance. It might even be that people are open to the use of GMOs to control pests such as cane toads in Australia. The main thing is that widespread acceptance of GMOs seems to occur case by case and when there are obvious advantages not available by other means.

This last point has implications for the potential use of GMOs in food production. The increasing risks to agriculture posed by climate change and population growth have led some people to call for greater use of GMOs in the food supply in order to deliver healthy and nutritious foods to people who have no access to unmodified alternatives. Sceptics, especially those favouring so-called natural products, question why we should turn to GMOs when better and more equitable forms of conventional agriculture might solve the world's food problems without any of the potential hazards associated with GMOs.

Today, the primary frontier concerns the labelling of GMOs: consumers are pushing for the right to know, and a number of commercial interests, among them Monsanto, are arguing against labelling that details the presence of GMOs in products. This ties in with the subject of supply-chain management: if GMOs are used at any point in the supply chain—for example, feeding a farm animal—should this be disclosed?

THE QUESTIONS

Are human beings part of the 'natural world'? If so, then what are the implications of this for the things we make? Can we trust scientists to create GMOs that are safe and genuinely useful? Can the risks be minimised and managed?

In particular:

- Do you know whether GMOs are present in the things you buy?

- Can GMOs be controlled so that natural stocks also remain available?

- Who has to bear the cost of *not* making GMOs?

- What kind of benefit would you require in order to become convinced of the case for using GMOs?

- Do you think of GMOs in the food supply chain as a special case? Are they more or less acceptable than other options?

× Where would you set the boundaries for what is done in connection with GMOs? Do you know enough of the relevant science to form a balanced view on this matter?

GLOBAL WARMING

The earth's climate is changing. The direction of that change (getting hotter) and its causes (including the substantial effect of human choices, mostly for the worse) are agreed by most. Considering what is at risk, you would think even the contrarians would urge prudence and back the consensus. The contrarians might prove to be right, something unlikely but possible, but if they are wrong the cost will be catastrophic — hence the argument for prudence.

As an ethical concern, global warming is about as profound as it gets. It is, as former Australian Prime Minister Kevin Rudd once noted, 'the great moral challenge of our generation'. In this instance politics trumped ethics, and Rudd's commitment to ethical action came undone. But Rudd was correct in his initial assessment of the ethical significance of this subject for several reasons:

× the need to balance competing 'goods' — prosperity, security, survival, justice and so on

× the effect on the planet as a whole — not just people but all of life

× the problem of collective action — whereby the benefits accruing from causing the problem and the costs of remedying it are asymmetrical and not fairly distributed

× the implications for future generations.

At every stage the ethical concerns multiply, shaping, and possibly restraining, the measures we might use not only to limit the damage but also to respond to what cannot be prevented. Climate change might well prompt mass migrations of people—not necessarily peaceful—as they search for safe and productive places to live.

Some people living in relatively affluent and developed countries might think they can pull up the drawbridge and remain safely locked away. Realistically, this will be an option only for the most self-sufficient of nations—armed and ready to protect their borders. But even these nations will end up being affected, no matter how much they want to turn away and isolate themselves from climate change's effects on the entire world.

Fortunately, however, the most dire of the predictions are not inevitable. Even better is the fact that ordinary people *can* make a difference. The trouble with global problems is that they sometimes seem overwhelmingly complex, and this can lead people to despair, because the problems seem too big, and then to withdraw. But every day offers scope for taking action to make a difference—from what we choose to buy to how we choose to vote, how we invest, and the conversations we have with our friends. We are all affected, so we all have legitimate reasons for becoming involved. Indeed, it is in our interest, individually and collectively, to do so and to embrace the opportunities that will inevitably present themselves.

The greatest opportunity seems to lie in the development of tech-nologies that will not only help limit global warming but also spur on innovation; an example is pursuing developments in renewable energy, such as distributed generation that eliminates dependence on just a few large suppliers. Innovation will, however, be far more pervasive than this, touching almost every area of life—building and construction, agriculture, transport, insurance and so on. Such profound change offers unprecedented opportunities to make fresh choices about how we design our societies. This means we could sweep away older patterns and forms of behaviour that no longer make sense. The global nature of the climate change problem will encourage us to look at the big picture in determining how we relate to other people and species.

Yet, although some people will be excited by such a huge challenge, others will be reluctant participants in what emerges. Not everyone will be an immediate winner. Some people will see their jobs disappear— and not just their jobs but also their whole way of life: think coal miners. Some people will have to move from where their ancestors have lived for millennia. This has happened before, with the rise and fall of sea levels occasioned by the natural cycle of ice ages, but historic precedent will offer little comfort to those forced into upheaval. We are going to need to make sure that people are not left behind as an exciting new world emerges from under the lash of necessity.

Climate change might be an inescapable fact of our collective future. It might turn out to present an extraordinary opportunity for humanity to reboot the way it lives. If this is so, the benefits will need to be equitably distributed so that everyone can make the transition in a condition that is both orderly and fair.

THE QUESTIONS

Climate change will threaten the viability of life on earth. What are our obligations to future generations? How do we ensure that the burdens and opportunities associated with change are equitably distributed?

In particular:

× Do you acknowledge an obligation to others and, if so, who counts in your considerations?

× What is the span of your influence and control? Do you purchase goods and services with climate change in mind?

× Are you optimistic about what might be done? Do you see climate change as presenting opportunities?

× Who might get left behind? What do we need to do to help people make the transition?

GOOD NEIGHBOURS

Although the majority of Australians live in self-contained homes with their family or friends, we nearly all live close to other people in their self-contained homes with their family or friends. Does living near someone make them a neighbour? Or is something else required?

There are many settings in which people live close to others they barely know. They might nod at each other when passing but apart from that have no contact at all. In these circumstances people can show themselves to be deeply resistant to the idea that they might be bound together by reciprocal obligations. It is as though proximity counts for nothing. Old people have been dead in their homes for weeks before being discovered. There have been people all around them, sometimes only metres away and separated by nothing more substantial than a few bricks, but nobody has noticed or, perhaps, cared to notice their absence. People have been brutally attacked, their screams piercing the night air, without anyone thinking to call the police or otherwise intervene.

Such events suggest that the difference between strangers and neighbours lies not in physical proximity but in an attitude of care for others. Normally, our capacity for care is directed towards those closest to us: it is far easier to connect with people who form part of our immediate environment. But one of the remarkable things about human beings is our ability to care about apparent strangers, often living a world away. The generous support Australians offer to aid and development agencies is evidence of this.

So how can we be indifferent to those immediately before us? Is it out of respect for their privacy? Is it out of fear of being caught up in the lives of others? Are we too busy? Or is it just an oversight—not seeing what is right in front of us?

Good neighbourhoods are reserves of social capital that can be drawn on for the sake of all. Children can feel, and be, safer when the entire community is available to see to their welfare. Criminals can feel, and be, at greater risk of detection. Public goods—such as shared gardens for fresh fruit and vegetables—can be created and sustained. Older people can be integrated into a community where their experience and wisdom can be drawn on to give strength to others.

It seems that the hallmarks of being a good neighbour are to notice people, to care a little, and to offer to become involved if necessary. There does not need to be any formal obligation of reciprocity, although this is often assumed.

THE QUESTIONS

Many of us live close to others; they can be neighbours in name yet not in substance. What might we need to do to enjoy the benefits and share the burdens of creating good neighbourhoods?

In particular:

- Is it possible to create a community event that might bring together people in the neighbourhood?

- Would it be worth producing a map of your immediate neighbourhood—who lives where, an inventory of experience and skills, an indication of preferences for community or privacy?

- Is there an understanding about who neighbours might call on for help if required?

- Do you prefer privacy or involvement with others? Is this a matter of choice or necessity—a busy life, competing commitments, and so on?

- What are the boundaries neighbours need to respect? How should those boundaries be defined and enforced? Where do the boundaries of a neighbourhood begin and end—a building, a street, a precinct? What if people wish to be included but fall outside those boundaries?

GOOD PEOPLE DOING BAD THINGS

There are in the world individuals who are deliberately nasty and destructive. They are, however, in the minority. The uncomfortable fact is that most of what goes wrong in the world is a result of good people doing bad things. They do not intend the harm they cause and are usually dismayed when confronted by the effects of their actions. Yet they *are* the cause.

The explanation is simple, really. Many people go about their life giving little thought to connecting what they do every day to any explicit framework of values and principles. Instead, they follow precedents, 'go with the flow' or act in accordance with long-established habits. Much of what guides current conduct made good sense when first developed. But times change, new circumstances arise, and old habits can become forces for ill rather than good. It takes only a moment to think of examples of this. Consider old habits of personal hygiene, such as an aversion to washing or the use of open cesspits, and how they had to change once it became clear that they contributed to epidemics of one kind or another. Science revealed the underlying causes of such epidemics, which included the practices of innocent people.

Good people can, however, avoid doing bad things if they *think*. At times, though, even that might not be enough. Some systems care little for what individuals think; they are indifferent to personal codes of ethics. These systems, which are all a product of human choice, can shape the actions of good people to bad ends — unless the good people challenge and force change to the system so that it becomes grounded in solid ethical foundations.

Once that is done — and it is difficult but possible — we need only worry about those who choose to be evil.

THE QUESTIONS

Few people intend to cause harm; indeed, most are remorseful when they inadvertently do. The challenge is not to 'drift' into this condition, like a sleepwalker who cannot see the edge of the cliff.

In particular:

× Are you a creature of habit? Are your habits appropriate to the world you live in or hope to make?

- ✗ Can you consciously attach the choices you make to an explicit framework of purpose, values and principles?

- ✗ Are you working within a system that overrides your choices or prompts you to do things you believe to be wrong? How might this system be challenged and improved?

- ✗ Do you think before you act?

HAVING A JOB

First, what exactly is a 'job'? And am I obliged to have one? Large numbers of people who are not employed by anyone make a major contribution to the community. Consider the contributions made by parents who choose to stay at home, family carers of the sick and infirm, or artists who enrich our society's cultural and intellectual life. None of these people might be paid for the work they do, but each could be said to be doing a vitally important job.

So the real question is, 'Do I have an obligation to make a positive contribution to the society I live in?' Part of the answer to this depends on how an individual might think about the purpose of their life. Does the person have latent talents that could be developed? What loss to the individual, or to the world, might there be if those talents are never exercised? Then there are questions of opportunity. People with remarkable capacities can be born into conditions that will never allow them to realise their potential. No matter how much they might want to develop, no matter how much they might try, they might be locked into a cycle of poverty or oppression such that every attempt to expand their personal horizons is crushed by grinding necessity.

And what about social obligation? Does each of us need to contribute to the maintenance or improvement of our society, using whatever abilities we have? Here the question is one of reciprocity. Why should others strive to make a good society, one from which each individual benefits, while others accept the benefits without lifting a finger to help? How can that be fair, especially if the opportunities to contribute are freely available?

These are the kinds of questions that help shape government policies. The most enlightened of these policies assume that every person has a contribution to make to society and then define ways to facilitate that contributing. Some people, however, grow up in hopelessness, believing it is futile to make an effort, and a few are simply content to sit back and let others carry their load.

THE QUESTIONS

Each person has the capacity to make a contribution to the world they live in. Many of these contributions go unrecognised because they are not classed as a 'job'. What might be done to encourage and support every person in making the most of their latent talents? And how should we respond to those who choose not to do so?

In particular:

- Are we giving adequate credit to those who contribute to society in non-monetary ways—for example, through the quality of their citizenship or their creativity?

- Should every person be forced to do something useful with their life?

- How do we uphold the dignity of those who are genuinely limited in their capacity to make a contribution?

- Should each person be allowed to develop their own talents? Or should people bend to meet the needs of society?

HOMELESSNESS

It is widely understood that if humans are to have any chance of flourishing they need a minimal degree of food and shelter. To be exposed to the elements in all weathers is to be exposed to discomfort, disease and ultimately an early death. It is for this reason that developed societies often focus on providing shelter for those forced onto the streets as a result of misfortune, domestic violence, accident or some other factor. For some people, being homeless can even be less of an evil than remaining with someone who is brutal or abusive.

It is simple enough to imagine what it might be like to be without shelter. Pick any night when it is cold and raining, and imagine yourself without cover, warmth or personal security. Now imagine that you are with your children or that you are suffering from a mental illness, afraid and confused. On what basis, other than free choice, should anyone in our society find themselves out in the cold?

Sometimes friends and relatives can provide shelter; sometimes it must be provided by the community as a whole, acting through agencies of the state. But there is a big difference between having shelter and having a home. A home is a place in which to relax, to make memories and to create meaning—to grow a little.

THE QUESTIONS

Although we might agree that all members of our society are entitled to shelter, should we also ensure that all have a home?

In particular:

- When it comes to having shelter (or, better yet, a home), what would you expect for yourself or your loved ones?

- What are the minimal conditions needed to make a home?

- Should the initial burden of responding to homelessness fall on families and friends? Or is this a community obligation?

- How does homelessness rank as a matter of importance for society? Are there other things that should be accorded higher priority?

HUMANS VIS-À-VIS OTHER CREATURES

Humans are endowed with the capacity to be free of the demands of instinct and desire and to make conscious, ethical choices. Every human being—no matter what his or her individual circumstances—experiences this form of being. Other creatures might well have the same capacity, but we do not know the extent to which this might be the case.

At first glance, this capacity would seem to place humans in a superior position vis-à-vis the rest of nature. To be different, however, does not necessarily mean being better. For example, the philosopher Epicurus and his followers believed that all beings are made from the same basic material (atoms) and that no particular form is better than another since the variety that is evident is just a matter of accident. Australian philosopher Peter Singer argues that any creature with a capacity to form preferences in a manner similar to humans should be treated as equivalent and therefore be regarded as a person—a being with full rights and responsibilities.

This line of thinking runs deeper than the question of humans' cruelty to animals. For example, many religious people believe that humans are made in the image of god but oppose any form of cruelty to other creatures. To be opposed to cruelty to other beings does not mean that all creatures stand on the same rung on the ladder of being.

The fact that we humans are capable of considering our ethical obligations to other creatures is, in itself, extraordinary. It seems this capacity is an emergent property of the universe—that self-consciousness is important in and of itself and not just because humans claim it is important. This might not make humans better than any other form of life, but it does make us distinctive and significant.

THE QUESTIONS

Humans share the planet with many other types of creatures. We tend to assign privilege to our position, reducing other creatures to the status of a resource available to satisfy our human wants and needs. Would the world be fundamentally changed—perhaps for the better—if humans saw themselves as being just one strand in the web of life?

In particular:

- Is there really anything distinctive about human beings that might justify a claim to superior status? If so, have we merely selected factors that suit our case for superior status?

- In view of our relative ignorance of how other creatures think and feel, should we err on the side of generosity and assume they are equal to us?

- Are we aware of the implications of equality? Would this bring an end to the use of other creatures for food, clothing, medical research, and so on? Is that a cost we should bear?

⨍ What lessons can be learnt from the natural world? If we were to apply those lessons, would humans' effect on other creatures be more beneficial or less deleterious? Is the natural world a kinder, gentler place, or is it, as Tennyson would have it, 'red in tooth and claw'?

ILLEGAL DOWNLOADING

Imagine you are walking along the street and you notice an elderly person fumbling with something in their pocket. Something falls to the ground. The elderly person fails to notice their loss and moves on. A moment later you come across a crumpled envelope and you find it is full of money. Do you claim the money as your own? Do you rush after the person and return their money to them? I have asked thousands of people this question over the years—young, old, rich, poor—and the answer is always the same. They return the money. Furthermore, they say that to keep it would be 'stealing'.

When you ask people why they make this decision they provide simple and obvious reasons. First, they know the money is not theirs. Second, they know the identity of the true owner. Third, the true owner's predicament is a matter of accident: they have done nothing to warrant their loss. Fourth, it is not difficult to return the money; indeed, people are determined to return it, even if they are told the rightful owner is wealthy and not especially pleasant.

You can take the same basic facts and apply them to cases of illegal downloading and obtain a completely different result. People know the material they download is not theirs. They know the identity of the true owner. They know the creator or owner of the material has done nothing deliberate to occasion the loss. Yet the material is downloaded without payment. By any measure, illegal downloading is stealing. How do people try to justify this?

One reason they give relates to the degree of difficulty in doing what is right. People I have spoken with assume that a digital product should be widely and instantaneously available around the world. Seeing no good reason for selective releases, illegal downloaders will often 'punish' a distributor who has sought to deny them immediate access. It is claimed that if the desired material were easily available at a reasonable cost people would be far more likely to pay. The growth of streaming platforms such as Netflix and Spotify seems to confirm this is a well-founded claim.

A second reason given for illegal downloads is based on the belief that large companies can afford the loss. This is similar to the attitude some people take to the theft of insured items—that insurance companies rather than individuals bear the loss. Such an approach is also linked to the perception that digital products cost something (sometimes a lot) to make but very little to replicate and distribute. People therefore question what is fair reward for, say, a song that can be spread around the world with little or no extra effort on the part of the artist or distributor.

This attempt to justify illegal downloads fails, however, at the point where the interests of most artists are taken into account. Only a few artists earn large incomes; the rest depend on being remunerated fairly for their creative work. There is thus sympathy for the plight of artists and a desire that they be fairly paid—if only there were a simple means for doing so.

In summary, people who use illegal downloads tend to know they are stealing. They are less likely to do it if the material is otherwise immediately available in a convenient form and at a reasonable price; failing that, the companies releasing the material are considered fair game. Finally, the risk of being caught is perceived to be relatively low, so there is not much deterrence in compliance programs.

THE QUESTIONS

In what circumstances, if any, is it acceptable to deny a creator or owner of digital material fair remuneration for their efforts by downloading their work without payment?

In particular:

× How would you feel if you depended on digital products for your income?

× How would you feel if someone stole part of your remuneration?

× Would you be proud to publicly discuss your approach to downloading material?

× What do you consider fair remuneration for digital products?

× To what extent is your behaviour shaped by the perceived risk of being caught?

INDIGENOUS AUSTRALIANS AND SPECIAL RIGHTS

By the time Europeans arrived in Australia, Indigenous Australians had been in occupation for at least fifty thousand years, during which they had developed trade routes, sustainable farming practices, aquaculture, and a mosaic of land tenure and law. This is not to say that Australia was an idyll of the noble savage the Europeans used to fantasise about. Indigenous Australians also waged war and used capital punishment and other kinds of violence. The point is that, whatever legal fictions the Europeans might have developed to suit their purposes, they did not find *terra nullius*, an empty land.[17]

---

17 One of the ironies of history is that the people of the United Kingdom who came to Australia had their own long history of dispossession—by Romans, Vikings, Normans (also Viking) and

It takes only a modicum of imagination to begin to see the situation from the perspective of the Aboriginal and Torres Strait Islander peoples. They had been living in some of the most beautiful and productive country in the world. No wonder they were incensed when strangers claimed the land for their own. No wonder there was violence. The British brought with them superior firepower and, unwittingly, a secret weapon—germs. Their incursions were greatly assisted by the disease and death their germs caused, and the result was that the Indigenous peoples were defeated. Their lands were forfeited to the victors in a process that had been occurring the world over among non-indigenous and indigenous peoples alike.

If only there had been a settlement rather than an invasion. If only the fighting had led to a stalemate rather than an overwhelming victory for the British. Then Aboriginal and Torres Strait Islander sovereignty might have been recognised rather than being buried under the doctrine of *terra nullius* or the conventions of conquest.

Despite this, the Australian legal system has latterly recognised that Aboriginal rights were not entirely extinguished upon the arrival of the Europeans. It is important to note that it was British law (as received and developed in Australia), and not Indigenous law, that lay behind decisions in cases such as *Mabo*.[18] Indeed, there are arguments that Aboriginal and Torres Strait Islander sovereignty might have survived colonisation and Federation, lying inoperative in the same way certain state laws lie inoperative (but not repealed) if they are inconsistent with legislation enacted by the Commonwealth parliament.

---

among themselves (English versus Irish, English versus Welsh, English versus Scottish).
18 See Mabo v Queensland (1992), High Court of Australia, http://www.austlii.edu.au/cgi-bin/sinodisp/au/cases/cth/high_ct/175clr1.
html?stem=0&synonyms=0&query=title+%28+%22mabo%22+%29.

The question modern Australia faces is to do with how we might best acknowledge the fact of first settlement by Indigenous peoples and ensure that their special status as the continent's First Peoples is recognised. Is this best done in the Australian *Constitution*, along with removing provisions that allow for racial discrimination? Is it best done by way of a treaty? If a treaty, with whom and by what means? (There are hundreds of autonomous Aboriginal and Torres Strait Islander political and cultural units, as opposed to one political body legitimately representing all Indigenous peoples.) What should be the status of Aboriginal and Torres Strait Islander customary law? Should it still apply in some cases, or has it become inoperative to the extent that it is inconsistent with the laws of the States and the Commonwealth? Should Australia's Indigenous peoples have special rights not available to other citizens? If so, will this be divisive, or is it justified by the need to compensate Indigenous peoples for historic wrongs? Would we be better served by a regime of common rights not qualified by matters of race or culture?

THE QUESTIONS

There is no doubt that the arrival of Europeans in Australia disturbed, and in many cases destroyed, the lives of Aboriginal and Torres Strait Islander peoples. How might this fact be acknowledged and what are its implications? Is it enough to say that Indigenous peoples 'got here first', or are there deeper questions of justice to be resolved?

In particular:

× Does 'first settlement' confer special rights?

× Are the costs of dispossession, often by force, a matter for just compensation? Is 'dispossession' merely another word for 'stealing'? Do the rules relating to individual theft not apply when states and entire peoples are involved?

× Does a final reconciliation with Aboriginal and Torres Strait Islander peoples represent a huge opportunity for all Australians to become integrated into the unbroken story of this continent, as held in trust by Indigenous Australians?

× To what extent should non-Indigenous people use their moral imaginations to relate to the experience of Indigenous people (and vice versa)?

× Is the concept of equal rights consistent with special rights for some? Where else do we afford special rights not available to the community as a whole; for example, priests enjoy special privileges, as do the churches to which they belong?

INTERNET DATING

I remember the panic I used to feel when asking a girl to go out with me for the first time. Indeed, I remember being 'kidnapped' by a couple of so-called mates who threatened to not return me to the school boarding house where I was living until I phoned a particular girl to ask her out. It was a matter of making the call or getting into strife back at school. I chose the lesser evil and phoned the girl. An 'awkward' call is the best way to describe it. I would have given anything for the relative anonymity of the internet, where you can take easy steps without being too exposed.

Of course, that's the upside of the internet—along with the fact that it is now possible to meet a vastly increased number of people. On the downside are false identities ('catfishing'), predatory behaviour (more 'catfishing') and a possible disregard for relationships because it is now far easier to pick them up and put them down. And then there is the Ashley Madison phenomenon whereby married people are enticed with the motto 'Life is short. Have an affair'. Finally, there is Tinder, not so much a dating site as a 'hooking-up' site whereby the possibility of developing an ongoing relationship comes a distant second to more immediate, and primal, objectives.

Some people never allow their relationship to develop beyond the online phase, engaging in a 'virtual' relationship (which can include 'remote' sex without ever physically meeting). And some people fall in love online, meet and live happily ever after.

If you plan to use the internet in the hope of striking up a relationship, never give relative strangers your last name, email address, street address or any other identifying information. And, if you are planning to meet someone for the first time, let someone else know where you are going and when you expect to return.

THE QUESTIONS

Is there a possibility of deception, such as in the case of the 'Cyrano effect', where a gifted writer can seduce someone through the use of 'true sentiments' linked to a false identity? At its best, this can be embarrassing or degrading; at its worst, it can be dangerous, especially when used as a technique by sexual predators to groom potential victims.

In particular:

- Are you being honest—with yourself and others online?

- What reasons do you have for trusting people you meet online? What steps might you take to build trust?

- Are your actions consistent with creating an online environment that is safe and respectful? Do you 'call out' others who behave badly?

- Would you be happy if what you are doing became known to people you respect and admire?

- Do you treat people online with the same consideration as you would show if face to face? Or do you exploit relative anonymity to your own advantage—and at a cost to others?

JOKES

Passing through Singapore's Changi Airport, I came across an unexpected multicultural gathering. From what I could see, people from very diverse religious, cultural and ethnic communities had come together and were, as one, having the time of their lives. Despite their differences, they had joined together in one of the most elemental and disarming behaviours of human beings—laughter. Sitting together in rows, they were responding to a common source, a television screening an episode of Rowan Atkinson's *Mr Bean*.

Most of Atkinson's humour is mimed, so the language barrier was not there. The group saw in Mr Bean a reflection of the simple foolishness of which every person is capable. Laughter filled the room.

Most importantly, though, there was nothing mean or nasty about Atkinson's creation. This can be contrasted with forms of humour that are based on making fun of others. In some cases, when directed against the powerful, such humour offers a tonic to society: satire is a very effective weapon when deployed against dictators and others who seek to rule by fear or intimidation. Any totalitarian regime fears ridicule as much as revolution; indeed, they often amount to the same thing.

But jokes can also be directed against the marginalised and powerless, and the effects of this can be devastating. 'I was just joking' is a familiar excuse offered by someone who is challenged for making fun of a vulnerable person, targeting perhaps their ethnicity, gender, sexuality, body shape or language skills. The trouble is the person who is the butt of the joke has no say in the matter: they are just being exploited for self-aggrandisement and the entertainment of others. Some people simply brush off the humili-ation, pretending it does not matter, but this veneer of indifference can hide a deeper wound.

It's different when people make fun of themselves. We are all entitled to do that. And some jokes—dark, or gallows, humour—can make terrible moments bearable, usually when the joke represents a form of solidarity among those who are suffering. The difference arises when people try to turn the suffering of others into an opportunity for selfish advancement, to be the centre of attention, to look good in the eyes of others. This is exploitative.

What, then, might our obligations be if we encounter a racist or sexist joke? Do we turn a blind eye? Do we join in? Do we challenge the joker? As a rule, there is no obligation to step in; that is something for an individual to decide, depending on how brave they feel and whether they face a risk if they speak up. We need to remember, however, that bad things can happen when good people do nothing.[19] At the very least, each of us needs to make a conscious decision about whether or not to reward a joke with a laugh.

THE QUESTIONS

What are the proper boundaries for humour? If we are committed to free speech where should we set our own boundaries?

In particular:

- Is this joke asking us to laugh with or at someone?

- How will the butt of the joke feel about this use of humour? Are they being exploited by others?

- Is the person being joked about a legitimate target for humour — for example, someone with unwarranted power?

- How would you feel if you were the one being joked about?

- Will this form of humour unreasonably burden others?

- Is such a joke consistent with your own ideas about who you want to be as a person at their best?

- If there is something wrong about the joke, should it be challenged? By someone else or by you? What are the risks? There is no need to expose yourself to harm, even if this might be the 'heroic' thing to do.

---

19 Edmund Burke is often quoted as having said, 'All that is needed for the triumph of evil is that good men do nothing.' This is disputed, however. If he did not say it, then he owes a debt of gratitude to Sir R Murray Hyslop of Kent, England, who in 1920 apparently credited Burke with such a profound insight.

LEGALISING DRUGS

Clarity of mind and the capacity to alter the mind's state have long preoccupied humans. Some people consider human consciousness and rationality to be the pinnacle of nature's achievement, either a divine gift or the product of evolution. The idea of the ability to alter the brain's chemistry, and thus the content of the mind, unsettles some people, and this concern is exacerbated when drugs prompt the unleashing of a dark side of human nature—especially violence unchecked by the ethical framework that constrains the more clear-headed. Add to this the fear of addiction and other forms of mental illness and mind-altering substances can be seen as an assault on the individual's autonomy.

Even so, elites have often used drugs—perhaps in the belief that they have a superior capacity to use them responsibly—while banning their supply to the hoi polloi. For example, in the 1920s the authors of Prohibition in the United States were often partial to a tipple. The same phenomenon occurred when the British aristocracy closed down the infamous 'gin palaces' while happily quaffing vast quantities of wine. Those acts of control were often driven by a kind of 'moral panic', usually associated with the belief that the 'lower orders' were rising above their proper station in life. This panic then transmuted into a question of law and order, as has happened more recently with the so-called war on drugs.

The overwhelming medical evidence is, however, that the risks associated with drug use are best understood as a health concern. Furthermore, disinterested expert opinion has it that trying to deal with the risks from a law and order perspective has been an expensive failure.

From time to time certain drugs have been labelled as especially dangerous to individuals and the community. The latest in a list that has previously included cannabis and cocaine is crystal methamphetamine, known as 'ice'. As Dr Alex Wodak of St Vincent's Hospital in Sydney advises:

> Methamphetamine is very similar to dexamphetamine. In the USA doctors can prescribe both drugs (but in Australia doctors can only prescribe dexamphetamine). Seventy per cent of people using methamphetamine in Australia use it less than once a month.

Not everyone who takes ice becomes violent or psychotic. The context of their lives matter. Dr Wodak notes, 'Most of the research is done in the USA where they have a blind spot for social and economic factors (poverty, childhood trauma, unemployment, poor education).'

This is not to say that ice should be legalised. The better option is to create a regulated market, starting with drugs that are less likely to cause problems for those who use them. This is to choose the lesser evil, in which regulated access to weaker stimulants reduces demand for more powerful alternatives, thus restricting the opportunities for traffickers to profit from addiction.

Finally, it should be noted that substances once considered equally dangerous have been found to offer considerable benefit when used under medical supervision; examples are a range of opiates and cannabinoids.

THE QUESTIONS

Considering that most drugs can do both good and harm—and that regimes based on total prohibition have never succeeded and can do much to sustain organised crime—would it be best to legalise all drugs and make them available under medical supervision and/or through a regulated market, such as applies to the sale of alcohol and tobacco?

In particular:

× Is it true that the so-called war on drugs has been a failure? What counts as good evidence to settle this question?

× Is recreational use of drugs a matter of personal liberty?

× How does society accommodate the harm to innocent third parties caused by drug use?

× How do we make sense of the fact that some drugs with potentially lethal effects—such as alcohol and tobacco—are legally available but others are not? Is there a rational basis for this distinction?

× Will greater access to all drugs lead society as a whole to be more responsible with their use?

× Are some drugs just too dangerous to be made available? Who should decide this? And on what evidence?

× If you were able to vote on the question of legalisation tomorrow, how would you vote?

× What age limits should apply to access if drugs were legalised?

× Police will need to be involved for as long as there are restrictions on drug use, so why not play safe and maintain a blanket ban?

× If drugs are legalised what penalties should apply to those who operate in the black market?

× Should free facilities for testing the pharmaceutical quality of all drugs be widely available in order to minimise the harm caused by adulterated products?

LYING

In general, human societies flourish in conditions of openness and truthfulness. This is because such societies can innovate and evolve on the basis of informed decision-making and high levels of trust— which is always more efficient than relatively costly and cumbersome systems of regulation and surveillance. There could, however, be a few situations in which deliberate falsehood might be permitted:

× when a person makes it plain they have no desire to know the truth

× when a person has no legitimate right to know the truth—for example, an enemy spy during a time of conflict

× when the effect of telling the truth would potentially harm innocent people.

Some people will object to these exceptions. For example, some Kantians insist that the truth must always be told, regardless of the consequences. More generally, though, Kantians will accept that maxims might be formed with enough precision to allow these exceptions to apply—not out of regard for consequences but as consistent with duty.

The thing that is to be noted about the exceptions is that they do not allow lies to be told for reasons of self-interest. Governments and political parties, in particular, should be mindful of this: too often they engage in deception by claiming something is in 'the public interest' when in fact they seek only to advance their private or personal interests. It is easy to rationalise falsehood and by doing so develop habits of mind that progressively normalise avoidance of the truth among individuals and in society at large.

THE QUESTIONS

We are all aware of the concept of the white lie, which is generally taken to mean a falsehood that is inconsequential and is usually told in order to avoid causing hurt. But if the flourishing of society ultimately depends on truthfulness is there a basis for better defining the conditions under which a lie can be told?

In particular:

× Is your lying primarily motivated by self-interest? For example, are you just trying to avoid the consequences of your actions?

× Do you need to tell an outright lie? Could you just remain silent?

× Is there any real difference between telling a complete lie and offering a half-truth through equivocation or 'mental reservation'?[20]

× Is your intention to tell the truth offset by other duties—such as the avoidance of causing harm to others?

× What effect will your stance have on others? If you cannot give your reasons for falsehoods (national security, say) are you prepared to live with ignominy? What if other people follow your example without knowing the principled basis on which you acted?

---

20 Wikipedia (2017), 'Mental reservation', https://en.wikipedia.org/wiki/Mental_reservation.

THE SUNLIGHT TEST

We should do only those things we would be
proud to be seen doing by those whose opinions
we respect.

MARRIAGE

Despite statistics showing that more than 30 per cent of all Australian marriages end in divorce, people continue to tie the knot. If anything, marriage has become more popular as a civil institution, and same-sex couples are now seeking the same civic right to marry as heterosexual couples enjoy.

Yet marrying, or making another kind of lasting commitment, is the relatively easy part. More difficult is finding the person one wishes to make a commitment to. The search for a partner (or even a girlfriend or boyfriend) is usually laden with opportunities for error, embarrassment, rejection, sadness and sometimes outright humiliation.

Deeper problems can arise when your potential partner is bound by cultural or religious obligations that limit their freedom of choice. For example, my father was raised as an Anglican, but he fell in love with a Roman Catholic. At that time, he had to promise that any children of the marriage would be raised in the Catholic faith. Only then could the marriage proceed.

So what should couples do if their relationship is considered taboo by one or both of their communities? One obvious option is that the couple can make a new life together, cut themselves off from their past, and probably become estranged from family and perhaps friends. Such a choice can entail physical risk—for both—because some cultures place family honour before personal love, blood ties and even the law of the land.

Whatever one might think about beliefs, customs and practices of this nature, it would be reckless to counsel indifference and urge the couple to proceed with their relationship. Love might eventually conquer all but, as Shakespeare shows in *Romeo and Juliet,* reconciliation might come only in death.

In these cases context really matters, as does flexibility. For example, some communities cling more fiercely to their traditions than do others. Some will accept converts or some other form of compromise. Community expectations will test a couple's commitment to each other by exposing the extent to which they, individually or together, are prepared to set aside aspects of their past identity in order to forge something new—the relationship that will emerge.

Some cultures deal with challenges of the kind just outlined (including the risk of rejection) through the social institution of arranged marriages. The potential benefits are obvious. First, there is a clear and impersonal structure within which potential partners can be assessed and accepted or rejected without there being such a risk of personal hurt. Second, it is possible to ensure that there is an appropriate 'fit' with the prevailing cultural and religious norms. There are also downsides, though. Couples can be forced to enter into unsuitable matches. They might grow to love one another, but not all will. Second, arranged marriages can reinforce rigid social boundaries that an enlightened and harmonious society might be better without.

Of course, few of us encounter or choose potential partners whose family or community context present apparently insurmountable barriers. In an increasingly multicultural society, however, it is likely that there will be far more recognition and negotiation of difference. The key to managing this is for each person to begin with self-knowledge and a willingness to interact respectfully with the other. This does not mean one should abandon one's beliefs at the outset: instead, one should be certain, but slow to judge.

Finally, it is essential to know where your boundaries lie—those beliefs, practices, values and principles you consider non-negotiable, even for the sake of love. But it is love that is most likely to triumph in the end. There does not seem to be any logic to love; nor does it seem to respect cultural or religious boundaries. The ultimate ethical question concerns the sincerity with which you embrace the other as a complement to your best self.

THE QUESTIONS

Is your commitment to the other person sincere? Do you wish to commit to them as much for their sake as for your own? Are they truly free to enter into marriage or an equivalent commitment of their own accord?

In particular:

- Are the implications of the proposed marriage—the upsides and the downsides—understood and accepted by both parties?

- Is there recognition that a marriage constitutes a 'third' shared life—that the life of each person, as an individual, as well as the life of the marriage, will need to be recognised and honoured?

- Is this a partnership of equals—even if expected roles vary?

MENTAL HEALTH

Of all the diseases people fear, those affecting mental health are often considered the most frightening. This is because diseases affecting the mind ultimately affect our sense of identity. Humans preserve a sense of continuity in their life by using memories to construct an unbroken narrative from past to present. Imagine if the chapters in that narrative were progressively lost, distorted or placed in the wrong order. Would your sense of self survive? Consider how it might be to live in a world in which you have lost your ability to distinguish between what is real and what is imagined, a world of auditory or visual hallucinations that seem as real as the words here. Or imagine waking up one day to find you lack the energy to get out of bed and you are looking at the world through a tunnel shaped by the fog of depression. You cannot see any physical signs of limitation, so you begin to blame yourself. The higher your expectations of performance, the worse the sense of internal, personal failure—and the greater the risk of suicide.

Until relatively recently fears of this kind led society to hide away people with mental health difficulties. Advances in medical science now allow a much greater understanding of the physiological basis for mental illness. In turn, this has brought about a change in attitudes, such that we now realise people experiencing mental illness are no more responsible for their situation than those experiencing a physical illness. Mental ill-health is being brought out of the shadows of the asylums and into the light of modern scientific research and evidence-based policy responses.

There remain, however, some underlying questions to be resolved. How do we set the boundaries for what is judged tolerably normal and what is judged to be in need of redress? For example, where on the autism spectrum should we draw a line that acknowledges difference and recognises the (sometimes spectacular) gifts of people with a different set of mental attributes? Where do we draw the line for dysfunction? Do we let the majority set the standard, especially if the general ordinariness of the majority could be blinding us to the remarkable in some individuals? Should such a line be drawn at all? How many people of genius—many of whom have changed the world for the better—have got away with being merely eccentric when if they were of lesser social standing they would have been at risk of being locked away as loopy?

Questions such as these will remain unanswered so long as aspects of mental ill-health remain taboo—sources of discomfort, embarrassment, and so on. Human health needs to be viewed as something that is integrated across body and mind, and across individuals and society.

In practical terms, the difficulties we most commonly face lie in dealing with people, often loved ones, whose mental health is at risk or in decline. Such situations can be linked to depression or dementia and can present as many challenges to carers as can physical illnesses. How one responds depends on a range of practical considerations, not least of which is the capacity of the individual concerned to cope in the world while managing their condition.

At the heart of many ethical systems is the idea of personal autonomy—the ability to make informed, rational decisions and then to give effect to them in the everyday world. This capacity is at risk in cases of mental illness, thus adding to the pressure on carers, whose scope of decision-making involves answering fundamental questions each person would normally be expected to answer for themselves. People charged with making these practical decisions have to exercise their authority in the interests of the individual on whose behalf they are acting. They might be required to do this even though they know the individual they seek to help would probably make different decisions were they free to do so.

THE QUESTIONS

How should we as individuals and as a society respond to mental illness? Should we allocate as many resources to develop and support the treatment of mental illness as we do to the treatment of physical diseases such as cancer? What is our personal responsibility when encountering mental illness in our own lives or among family, friends and associates?

In particular:

× Have we overcome our deep, cultural fear of mental ill-health?

× Are some variations in mental health within the community a bonus rather than a cost?

× What level of mental health does a person need in order to function in society? Who is to judge? And according to what criteria?

× Are we applying an integrated approach to physical and mental health? Are mental health services rational, integrated and based on good evidence?

× Are we as well equipped to care for people with mental illness as we are to deal with people suffering from physical illness?

MIGRATION AND NATIONAL BORDERS

Where you are born is largely a matter of luck. Some are born with good fortune; others are exposed to the gravest of risks through no fault of their own. Nature's borders are relatively few and are permeable (rivers, mountains, oceans and so on), so it is difficult to see how it would be just to require some people to live poorly when they could live well by simply crossing a border.

On the other hand, the prosperity some people enjoy can often be the product of creating and sustaining a sense of shared identity—and of limiting access to natural and social resources on a sustainable basis. A global open market in the movement of people might lead to the impoverishment of all. Borders might thus play a valuable role at the global scale.

The challenge is to ensure that those with plenty do not selfishly keep it all to themselves. If there is more of a good than a particular population can use, justice suggests that the surplus be shared with others who are in need. If some of those surplus goods can be enjoyed only by coming to the more fortunate country, the borders should be opened. To say that borders should be open is, however, not to say they should be unregulated. Nations prosper and remain peaceful if they run an orderly immigration program. Domestic populations understand the probable benefits of migration, but they need to have confidence in the management of the immigration process, so as to ensure that the inflow of people is sustainable and consistent with maintaining community harmony.

A further factor affecting patterns of migration is people's general preference for remaining 'at home', close to ancestors, family, friends and familiar natural and cultural landmarks if at all possible. The more peace and prosperity are widespread and general, the less pressure there is on borders. Nations that are more fortunate therefore have an interest in extending their luck to others.

Finally, something needs to be said about the preservation of social harmony, which is possible only with diversity. Countries such as Australia have flourished by deliberately inviting a range of diverse people to populate them. If this process is to work well, though, every citizen—whatever their place of origin—must adopt a number of common principles, such as the rule of law.

THE QUESTIONS

In view of the fact that one's place of birth and general life opportunities are largely a matter of luck, for the sake of justice should we do away with national borders? Or do borders play a useful role in the world—so long as they are managed equitably?

In particular:

× What would you hope to do with national borders if you did not know whether you were going to be born in a 'lucky' or an 'unlucky' country?

× How might you feel if the existence of borders would harm the prospects of your children or grandchildren?

× What is a fair basis for managing access to a fortunate country such as Australia?

× What conditions should migrants accept as the cost of maintaining social harmony in a host nation?

× How important is the sustainability of population growth? Could more people live in a country such as Australia if we all reduced our environmental footprint?

MOBILE PHONE ETIQUETTE

I was recently offered the opportunity to participate in a radio interview while heading out to western Sydney on a train. I refused. For one thing, I thought I would be considered, with good justification, a complete turkey: the last thing you need on a train is to be overwhelmed by the sound of someone blathering into their mobile phone—and you can't whisper on the radio.

This gives rise to a more general question: now that the world is awash with mobile phones, each with the power to deliver videos, games and messaging of all types, as well as the occasional call, what should be the ethical guidelines for their use?

The most obvious point is that, for all the technology's usefulness, it is self-defeating if it gets in the way of good communication. Central to this is paying attention to the person you are supposed to be communicating with. I have fallen into the trap presented by mobile devices. The very fact that they are there can be a distraction, even when they are not making noises. The seductiveness of instant information and instant connection can too easily draw you away from the immediacy of the moment. The result is a 'shadow version' of yourself in the room or at the table, or on the train, while the real you is, at least partially, somewhere else.

This notion of the shadow self is exploited by some people as a way of avoiding difficult situations. The most infamous examples involve stories of people ending intimate relationships by text message because they lack the courage to confront the other person. I realise that people used to end relationships by way of a letter, but this was usually a matter of necessity (for example, people being far apart) rather than choice. Whatever the technology, questions of honour and compassion remain.

Finally, there can be times when it is acceptable to use a mobile device when someone is speaking. I remember speaking to a group of people who seemed to be entirely focused on their devices, which offended me a bit until I realised that they had been looking up information about the points I was making. At least, that is what they told me.

THE QUESTIONS

When you use mobile technology are you respectful of other people and their needs—for quiet, for connection, for respect?

In particular:

- ˣ Is this the right context in which to use your mobile device? Is it reasonable to be using it here and now? Will your use have an adverse effect on someone with a legitimate right to be undisturbed by it?

- ˣ Is your use of your mobile device creating a shadow self— distracted and disengaged? Do the people you are with have a reasonable expectation that you will be entirely present?

- ˣ Are you using your mobile device as a shield to avoid unpleasant moments that you should otherwise confront?

- ˣ Are you using your mobile device as a weapon to harm others?

- ˣ Is the use of this device respectful to others?

OBLIGATIONS TO FRIENDS

There are various types of 'goods' in the world that are infinitely divisible. They are 'common goods', and counted among them is the 'good' of friendship. To take this idea further, consider a bowl containing a hundred chocolates. If someone takes fifty-one, that leaves just forty-nine to be divided between everyone else in the room. Imagine, however, that there are a hundred people in the room—all open to friendship. The fact that one person befriends ninety-nine others does not deny anyone else the opportunity to do the same thing. Everyone in the room can make ninety-nine friends. That is what makes friendship a common good. It can be enjoyed, in equal measure, by all.

Because we live in a world dominated by the economics-related idea that value (the price we are prepared to pay) is a function of supply and demand, we tend to undervalue common goods such as friendship. Yet each of us knows, through direct experience, that true friends are of inestimable value to our lives. We also know that, despite unlimited opportunities to make friends, we each have relatively few true friends in a lifetime.

A good friendship can be recognised in the fact that, even if you have not seen the person for ages, you are able to pick up where you left off, as if not a day has passed. Friends also come into their own in our moments of great need, materialising, as if out of nowhere, when required. This kind of thing is usually effortless and is never expressed in any formal agreement. Instead, there is a tacit under-standing between friends that they have particular obligations to each other. The following are among these obligations to our friends:

x being available when they need us

x being candid in terms of who we are and the advice we offer

x preferring their interests to those of others—unless to do so would be unjust

x helping them when asked—and offering help without being asked if their need is evident

× asking of them only what you would be prepared to offer, so that the relationship is based on equality and reciprocity

× taking personal risks for their sake.

THE QUESTIONS

How do we recognise the obligations we owe to friends (as opposed to acquaintances), realising that the value of friendship need not lie in its relative scarcity?

In particular:

× Are you open to making friends with people who are 'not like you'? Or do you look for friendship only within a narrow circle?

× Are you open and honest with your friends?

× Do you ever use your friends for your own advantage? Does your letting them know of your plans make this acceptable?

× Are you taking your friends for granted?

× Does it matter that some people have very few friends? Or is this just another form of variability in human affairs?

OTHER PEOPLE'S CHILDREN

There are occasions when children are not in the immediate care of their parents or when other adults are present to observe their behaviour. At these times a non-parental adult might be tempted to intervene, either to direct a child's behaviour or even to rebuke or punish a child for behaviour the adult deems improper.

In extended families, where a community of adults might share in a general responsibility for child-rearing, this might not be a problem. Since the advent of the nuclear family, however, parents might be affronted by the idea that others should assume a role in raising their children. This can be especially problematic if parents have made a conscious decision not to adopt the practices they experienced as children at the hands of their own parents.

Context matters — especially the degree of agreement about who has a legitimate right to be involved in shaping the lives of children. For example, if you belong to a family where it is considered normal for child-rearing to be a shared responsibility, then you might assume that it is generally acceptable to be involved with other people's children. You might even count on other adults to look out for your children. This is fine if everyone agrees on the range of obligations. It can, however, pose considerable difficulties when mixing with others who embrace a narrower set of parental boundaries.

Close family ties might be thought to give rise to a greater likelihood of involvement, but this cannot be assumed. Instead, the best approach is to seek explicit agreement, including in relation to the values and principles the parents wish their children to learn and the boundaries they apply when it comes to discipline. In general, the safest bet is to talk to the parents directly. If their children are behaving badly the parents should be informed and should take responsibility for dealing with the situation. If they do not take on that role they might fall into the category of 'difficult' friends or relatives.

Finally, there is one exception to the general principles just outlined. If it is a matter of immediate concern for the health and safety of a child, adults must intervene, even if in doing so they act in a manner inconsistent with the wishes of the child's parents.

THE QUESTIONS

Modern Western societies tend to assume that children are the responsibility of their parents. This is not necessarily the case in other cultural settings, where child-rearing can be a shared responsibility. Parents might also want to break with the patterns of the past, instilling new values and principles in their children; for example, they might reject the use of corporal punishment, despite having received it from their own parents. Who then decides the span of control to which children might be exposed?

In particular:

- Have you placed your children in the care of others? If so, did you make the boundaries clear?

- Is it fair to expect others to be just like you when it comes to discipline? Grandparents, for example, are famous for indulging their grandchildren ... and then sending them home. Is this not part of the pattern of the ages? Does it matter enough for you to intervene?

- Should the parents of the children involved in the unacceptable behaviour be asked to resolve the situation, no matter what?

- Should children be given special licence to be boisterous and annoying—as part of being a child? Are the days gone when a child was supposed to be 'seen and not heard'?

- Do all the adults present understand and share the same views about child-rearing? If not, how can these differences be made explicit?

PARENTHOOD: YES OR NO?

There is a widespread assumption that most couples will at some stage want to have children. This applies not just to heterosexual couples but also to same-sex couples offering a stable basis for family life. It also needs to be acknowledged, though, that some couples will be unable to have children or will choose not to do so.

Couples that choose not to have children often cite ethical reasons for their choice—for example, an aversion to bringing children into a world with so many deep-seated problems or a belief that the planet is already overpopulated with humans and that they do not want to make a bad situation worse. The availability of widespread and effective contraception makes the decision not to have children a far more practical option than is the case when, for cultural or religious reasons, contraception is unavailable or rarely used.

For the majority of people wanting to have children, however, there are ethical questions that go beyond those to do with population levels and so on. The most obvious of these concerns our capacity to sustain children in conditions that will allow them to flourish. Thinking about this forces us to consider whether we are being selfish—wanting children solely to satisfy our own needs. None of this is to suggest that we might not come to love our children for their own sake: it is just that we live in times when we have a choice about having children, and we need to examine our motivation.

Then there is the question of how many children to have and what to do, if anything, about family balance. In our case, my wife and I were fortunate to have a 'pigeon pair'—a son and a daughter. We had thought we might have four children, but we stopped at two, confident that we could manage the costs (not just financial) of giving them both the best possible start in life. Yet my wife and I both come from much larger families (five children in each), and our respective parents coped.

Finally, there is the predicament of people who are unable to have children even though they want to. In the past they would have remained childless or would have resorted to adoption as the way of building a family with children. They now have other options thanks to developments in assisted reproductive technologies (such as in-vitro fertilisation) that can allow many otherwise infertile people to have a child that is genetically their own.

Some individuals and communities oppose the use of assisted reproductive technologies on the basis that such practices are unethical. They might argue that all life is the gift of god and that human beings should not interfere with god's work. Other lines of argument are that embryos are sacred and should not be destroyed in the aftermath of IVF or that nature has not intended that certain people have children. Both objections are easily refuted by, for example, refusing to accept the existence of god or the 'personhood' of embryos, by acknowledging that science is part of god's work, or by observing that humans constantly interfere with nature—when, say, performing surgery or administering drugs as part of the everyday practice of medicine.

Assisted reproductive technologies come at a cost for the intended parents, though. This is not just a matter of money. The potential mother must participate in a program that can be painful and disturbing and does not offer a guarantee of a successful pregnancy. That is why responsible IVF programs insist on counselling for participants. But some couples are destined not to be able to raise their own offspring and need to accept the fact that, through no fault of their own, they will become parents only by way of adoption.

Their experience might be personally tragic, but it serves to remind us all that parenting is a privilege, not a right.

THE QUESTIONS

Under what circumstances is it right to accept the privilege of becoming a parent?

In particular:

× What are our real motives for wanting to have children?

× Do you have the capacity to look after the children you plan to have, affording them a reasonable chance in life?

× What costs are you willing to bear in order to become parents?

× Are there good reasons why in your case, or in general, it would be better not to become parents?

PERSONAL EMAILS AT WORK

Some people never, or only rarely, use emails at work. They might not need to, being involved instead in customer service, manufacturing or maintenance, or even out in the world working on farms, fishing vessels or drilling rigs. There are, however, many people who spend a considerable portion of their day using email as a tool for work. Sometimes it is also necessary or advantageous to send an email about something unrelated to work—to a loved one, to a child's school, to a travel agent … the list is long. Is it ethical to use a work email system for personal reasons?

People used to ask the same question about using the telephone at work. In general, the answer was simple: it depended on whether the employer allowed reasonable private use. Email makes things a bit more complicated, partly because there are two parts to an email service—the system that generates and receives messages and the network that carries the resultant traffic.

As part of an employment contract most modern workplaces include a stipulation that the employer will have unrestricted access to emails sent and received using their system. Although not much is generally made of this fact, there is rarely any such thing as a private email sent from work, even if it is entirely personal.

Considering that employers need to maintain an email system for their own purposes, the additional cost of employees sending the odd personal email is virtually nothing. But if employees make free use of the service, without restraint, data costs can grow considerably. It then becomes a trade-off between a loss of privacy for the employee and an affordable policy for the employer. In the end it is up to the employer to make clear what rules, if any, apply to people wanting to send personal emails on the work system, and employees should respect the rules.

THE QUESTIONS

To what extent should employees make use of their employer's email service for private purposes?

In particular:

* Does your employer have any explicit rules about the use of its email system for private purposes?

× Does your employer reserve the right of access to all emails sent and received using its system?

× Are you prepared to sacrifice your privacy for the ease and convenience of using your employer's email system?

× Can you use your own personal email address on your employer's network? If not, does your employer agree to your using a work email address? In this latter case, would your employer be happy to have their name associated with what you are discussing by email?

PETS

About 63 per cent of Australian households keep an animal as a pet.[21] This is one of the highest rates of pet ownership in the world, and the numbers are dominated by dogs and cats.

Animals have lived with people and in human communities since time immemorial. Some of them have done so involuntarily and would prefer to roam free if given the chance. Other animals, most notably dogs, have sought out human company and in doing so have developed a symbiotic relationship based on mutual trust and affection.

In view of this, it seems reasonable to see a degree of pet ownership as ethical — providing the conditions are not cruel and the essential nature

---

21 RSPCA (2016), 'How many pets are there in Australia', RSPCA Australia Knowledgebase, http://kb.rspca.org.au/How-many-pets-are-there-in-Australia_58.html

of the animal is not compromised. For example, there can be no justification for making large dogs live in tiny apartments without access
to a place where they can run and jump and stretch their legs. As for
keeping wild animals as 'trophy pets', if their survival in the wild is in
question it would almost certainly be better to help save their habitat.

There are, however, further things to consider when it comes to
the breeding and ownership of animals as companions. Many of
them have physical characteristics that humans see as desirable but
that are only present as a result of genetic mutations in the breed —
mutations that can cause otherwise avoidable pain and suffering
for the animal. This is most commonly the case with dogs, but the
world of cats also offers examples. In a paper presented to a scientific
seminar convened by the RSPCA in 2012, veterinarian Dr Richard
Malik cited the case of Scottish Fold cats:

> Scottish Fold cats have as their defining feature a
> forward folding of the pinnae. This gives them a unique
> look, which many people find particularly appealing.
> This fits in with the Lorenzian theory of beauty (named
> after the Nobel prize–winning ethologist), but suggests
> people find animal 'faces' appealing if they have
> forward facing eyes and floppy ears.
>
> It was soon discovered, however, that if Scottish Fold
> cats were mated to other Scottish Fold cats, many of
> the offspring developed a severe crippling lameness
> early in life. Cats so affected had shortened, malformed
> legs and radiographic abnormalities affecting the
> growth plates that could be readily appreciated. As a
> result of this discovery, the breed was outlawed by the
> Cat Fancy in the United Kingdom.[22]

---

22 RSPCA (2012), 'Proceedings of the 2012 RSPCA Australia Scientific Seminar', Canberra,
https://www.rspca.org.au/sites/default/files/website/The-facts/Science/Scientific-Seminar/
2012/SciSem2012-Proceedings.pdf

The nature of the burdens we impose on animal companions for the sake of satisfying our aesthetic preferences is an important ethical concern.

Finally, there is the question of what to do with pets that are unwanted or abandoned. National figures on this are not kept, but one study has estimated that in 2010 just under four hundred thousand cats and dogs were taken into Australian shelters,[23] the vast majority of them eventually being killed. And then there are associated considerations to do with the damage caused to Australian native wildlife by formerly domesticated and now feral animals—especially cats—and by other uncontrolled household pets.

THE QUESTIONS

Some animals seem to enjoy the company of humans just as much as humans enjoy theirs. They might choose to be with us. Considering that humans are ultimately in control of the animals' lives, however, how do we discharge our obligations in a manner that takes into account a range of competing interests?

In particular:

× Can this animal be kept in a condition that will allow it to flourish? Do I understand the nature of this animal and its particular physical and psychological needs?

× Am I making a selection on the basis of preferences that impose a burden on the companion animal? Is my choice supporting a breeding program aimed at creating animals destined to suffer from preventable genetic diseases?

× Am I willing to take responsibility for this animal for all of its life?

---

23 Getting to Zero (2010), 'Estimated number of dogs and cats abandoned and killed in Australia in 2009/10', http://www.g2z.org.au/pdf/Calculation%20of%20National%20Figures%20 09%2010%20incl.%20Healthy%20Treatable.pdf

× Can I control this animal so that it does not become a threat to other people or creatures?

× Do I understand how much money I am willing to spend for the sake of this animal?

× Do I understand and accept the implications of not paying for particular medical procedures for the animal—the most likely of these being having the animal's life brought to an end?

PORNOGRAPHY AND PROSTITUTION

English philosopher John Stuart Mill's famous aphorism on the principle of liberty and the exercise of power—'The only purpose for which power can be rightfully exercised over any member of a civilized community, against his will, is to prevent harm to others'[24]—is not just about restraining the power of the state. It is also meant to apply to the relationship between individuals. Indeed, it is designed to extend, to the greatest extent possible, the liberty of the individual. If any action is not harmful to others—whether or not formally proscribed—we ought to be free to take it.

This general approach is often invoked when it comes to sexuality and personal intimacy and is captured by the idea that governments (and others) should 'stay out of our bedrooms'. Despite this, though, the state has a long history of intervening in relation to prostitution and pornography. What should we think about the regulation of these areas of life?

The practice of prostitution has formed part of religious traditions, public services and private markets for millennia. Prostitutes,

---

24 Mill, JS (1975), 'On liberty', *Three Essays*, OUP, Oxford, UK.

courtesans, escorts, sex workers—whatever their name—have not always been considered immoral in either their person or their actions. At times they have been respected and admired. For example, in ancient Roman times the procuring of sexual services was considered perfectly normal. If prostitutes wore distinctive clothes it was not so much to shame them as to make them easier to identify. Later, in fifteenth century Rome, Vannozza dei Cattanei achieved great wealth and influence as the mistress of Cardinal Rodrigo Borgia (later Pope Alexander VI), to whom she bore four children, all of them acknowledged by their father.

Nevertheless, prostitution has been subject to a longstanding under-current of disapproval. Critics have warned of all manner of unde-sirable or antisocial outcomes—the disconnection between sexual pleasure and love, the risk of transmitting disease, an inability to manage family succession and the transfer of property, and so on.

Depictions of a sexual nature have a similarly long history, often being associated with higher arts and crafts. The ancient Greeks and Romans were notable exponents, but pornography predates their time and is a feature of many cultures, Eastern and Western. For example, some of the earliest images are the 'Venus' figurines and rock art dating back about twenty-five thousand years. Eastern art—for example, in the Indian *Kama Sutra*—has a similar erotic pedigree, albeit linked (as in the case of the Venus figurines) to religion and spirituality.

With both prostitution and pornography the central questions relate to consent and harm. Even if one is a libertarian in Mill's sense, to what extent can we assume that the people involved in sex work and pornography, who are predominantly women, have really made a free, informed choice about being involved? Would this work have been their first choice among a number of options or have they been driven by necessity or a need to boost their self-esteem through being desired? Or have they been forced into it?

We know that large numbers of sex workers are not involved as a matter of genuine choice and that many are trafficked and imprisoned in a system of sexual servitude. They are exploited and abused, experiencing treatment that is often worse than that meted out to animals. There are, however, some sex workers and people involved in the making of pornography who have genuinely made a free choice to do this work. These people might be relatively few in number, but they do exist.

So, if we imagine a world in which sex work and pornography are offered with the genuine consent of those involved and are 'consumed' by others who also freely consent, why might society feel the need to be involved?

This brings us to the second aspect of Mill's principle—to do with the harm that can be caused to others. The challenge critics of prostitution and pornography put forward concerns not just the fact that the industries are populated by too few people who have genuinely consented. It is also about the harm caused to individuals and societies, and the foremost of these claims is that the commodification of sex damages intimate relationships, especially those between younger people.

Research suggests that a growing number of people (male and female) are gaining access to pornography at a young age[25] and that what they observe is shaping their expectations about and understanding of

---

25 Many studies canvass the relevant statistics; see, for example, Oliva, L (2016), 'The impact of porn culture on girls is too big to ignore', *Feminist Current*, 14 December, http://www.feminist-current.com/2016/12/14/impact-porn-culture-girls/.

things such as body type, normal sexual behaviour, and the roles of men and women. Concern is amplified by the fact that some pornography involves non-consensual violent sex: even if it is just 'acting', such material tends to normalise behaviour that most societies would seek to prevent. Finally, the ubiquity of the internet is allowing pornography to have greatly increased reach and impacts in society.

Whether or not sex work and pornography cause harm to individuals or societies is an empirical question. If they turn people into sex 'objects', that can be determined by research. If that is found to be occurring, it is a major ethical concern because no person is supposed to be treated solely as a means to some other person's ends. In the meantime, the challenge is to balance a regard for individual liberty with a prudent, precautionary approach to harm prevention.

THE QUESTIONS

Sex is a largely private matter that should not be subject to interference from others. Commercial sex services and pornography are, however, offered just like any other commercial service, for private profit. Should the maintenance of public goods and principles such as respect for others be given greater weight in our deliberations?

In particular:

× To what extent are those involved in sex work and pornography making a genuinely free choice about their involvement? How can you know?

× In the absence of certainty about consent, should we assume the worst?

× What exactly counts as harm in our society? Are we informed in our assessment? What role might prejudice play?

- In the absence of certainty about harm, should we opt for liberty?

- Where should we look for guidance in such matters—science, religious authorities, common sense?

- Does the relative vulnerability of the young change the equation? Should special measures be taken to protect them?

- If a majority of participants are not genuinely free in their decision to be involved in pornography or prostitution, is it fair to limit the choices of the minority who are?

- If reform is necessary, who should pay for it—sex workers, pornographers or their clients? If the market is controlled, will this of itself bring about change for the better?

- Can technology help—for example, 'locking off' areas for consenting adults without affecting others? Is the risk too great if these measures fail?

POWER OF ATTORNEY AND THE MAKING OF WILLS

The quest for autonomy—the right to decide things for oneself and to act accordingly—has been bound up with the aspirations of individuals and groups for millennia. For groups, including whole societies, the concept is often expressed in terms of self-determination and has featured in political struggles such as those leading to independence from colonial masters. For individuals, the search has been for personal autonomy, a notion that has animated movements in pursuit of everything from freedom of religious and political expression to the availability of abortion.

Autonomy is therefore associated with the concept of liberty—in particular, a person's right to control decisions affecting their own self. In turn, this presumes that each individual is competent to make informed decisions. 'Competent' is typically taken to mean that the person has the presence of mind to weigh up arguments, to understand and evaluate evidence and, generally, to operate with a sound mind. In some circumstances this is not possible, either because the individual is suffering from a mental illness or because they are not able to speak directly for themselves. A person might be in a coma or a persistent vegetative state, for example, or they might have died having expressed a desire to have their wishes respected.

There are a number of options for dealing with these situations. If a person anticipates that they will be alive but unable to speak for themselves, they can prepare a 'living will', or an 'advanced care directive' in the case of prospective medical treatment. Such documents can be used to guide—and in some cases to bind—others who need to make decisions on behalf of the individual. Another option is to grant to someone 'power of attorney', authorising them to make decisions on your behalf. Naturally enough, granting power of attorney to another person is an act of trust: you would need to be utterly confident that the person receiving that power will always act in your best interests.

A will, or last will and testament, is a legal document that can be used, among other things, to direct how your property should be allocated after your death. The directions recorded in a will are usually, but not always, respected. In general, the law requires that the provisions of a will be fair to those most immediately connected with the person who made the will (family members in particular). Family matters are notoriously tricky: some families are torn apart by greed, envy, or a sense of rejection and injustice when property is redistributed after a death. Furthermore, it is not possible for the dead to compel the living to behave in a particular way. You might want to specify all manner of conditions for how your possessions are to be disposed of, but whether these conditions are honoured depends on their reasonableness and the regard with which your beneficiaries hold you in memory.

These matters are of importance not only for those growing older but also for much younger people within an extended family. Conversations about advanced care directives, the allocation of family assets, the effects of inherited wealth on children, and so on, are best addressed when those involved are all able to participate in the relevant discussions, without the immediate pressure that inevitably mounts and distorts judgment during periods of crisis.

THE QUESTIONS

There are two important questions when it comes to powers of attorney. Do you completely trust the person to whom you grant the power to act solely in your best interests? And are you sufficiently clear about what those interests are? Wills are much more complex, and the main thing to resolve concerns the need to be fair and constructive and being true to your own convictions.

In particular:

- Have I made my wishes—and my understanding of where my interests lie—clear to all concerned? Have I done this in writing if possible?

- Do I have good reasons for trusting the person to whom I propose to grant a power of attorney? What makes me confident that they will act in my best interests?

× In the case of a will, am I being fair to all concerned? Or am I using my will to 'get even' when, perhaps, forgiveness would be a better path?

× Does someone outside my immediate family have a legitimate claim on me? Are there undischarged debts and obligations that should be honoured?

× How can I avoid causing a breakdown in relationships, especially in my own family? Will my heirs be able to make the best use of their inheritance? If my children are already grown up and do not need goods or money, is it OK to leave money to my grandchildren without consulting their parents?

× Are there any family traditions or obligations in relation to disposing of things such as heirlooms that have been passed down through generations?

PUBLIC TRANSPORT

The freedom to come and go as one pleases, the ability to take control of one's life, the convenience of travelling from door to door—these are just some of the attractions of driving one's own car. In fact, the attractions are so great that they usually cancel out considerations such as cost, safety, pollution and community impacts.

Increasingly, we are being encouraged to use public transport. Governments put the case as a means of tackling congestion on the roads and reducing adverse environmental effects. It might also be that public transport offers a levelling experience, bringing people together though shared experiences. Insurance companies are also great champions of public transport: in their ideal world they would receive premiums for cars that are rarely on the road, thus reducing their risk of having to pay out on claims arising from accidents.

For most citizens, however, the central considerations are about ease of access, efficiency and reliability, and relative cost. Governments can advocate for public transport until the cows come home, but their pleas will fall on deaf ears if they fail to offer high-quality, affordable services.

There are also sound ethical reasons for citizens to consider public transport, where it is available. The collective goods governments seek to achieve—fewer cars on the roads, to help to reduce pollution; less congestion, to decrease the risk of injury or death from accident; and so on—are worth supporting. The trouble is that attainment of these collective goods requires some loss of individual autonomy, something realised in practice when behind the steering wheel of a car.

The second problem is that public transport is not equally available to all. Some citizens, usually communities with lower socio-economic status, are poorly served by public transport infrastructure. For these people a car is often the only reasonable option. This is supportable from an ethical perspective. As the German philosopher Immanuel Kant once noted, "'Ought' implies 'can'": we are not under any obligation to do the impossible. Where public transport is unavailable or is practically ineffective the use of private transport is acceptable. Of course, in such circumstances we should nevertheless aim to reduce the negative effects of our practices. This might involve things such as car-pooling schemes or driving to transport hubs.

Some of these problems might be resolved through technical innovation. For example, the deployment of electrically powered self-driving cars might reduce pollution and the risk of accidents—but with a loss of autonomy as human drivers are replaced by robotic systems. Indeed, it might be that developments of this kind, along with further development of the 'sharing economy', will ultimately blur the distinction between private and public transport.

For now, though, an increasing number of commuters have a clear choice.

THE QUESTIONS

In what circumstances should a commuter opt for public transport? Are the collective benefits of sufficient value to justify the sacrifice of private utility?

In particular:

- Is public transport available in a reliable, efficient and cost-effective form?

- Would taking public transport impose a genuine burden, consuming valuable time you could better use in other ways?

- Is any minor personal inconvenience compensated for by the extent of the public goods accrued by your use of public transport?

- Are you setting a good example by using public transport? Does it encourage others to do the same, thus helping to make the system as a whole more viable?

- Would it be a good thing if everybody used public transport where possible?

- If you need to use private transport could you make it more efficient by ride-sharing or in some other way?

RAISING CHILDREN

Despite the task of raising children being recognised as one of the most difficult and important undertakings a person can engage in during their lifetime, there is no process of preparation for it. Instead, parents are usually left to work things out as events unfold. The temptation, of course, is to replicate what we experienced at the hands of our own parents or perhaps to seek advice from friends, relatives and published material. When couples live close to their own parents or other relatives, the task of raising children can be shared, and new parents can benefit from the experience of older, wiser heads.

Following older patterns is not always a good idea, though, especially when past experience includes forms of parenting that were damaging to children or are out of step with contemporary values and principles and the requirements of modern society. That is why parents must always retain a critical perspective on the way their children are treated. It is neither safe nor responsible for parents to raise their children using methods that have no better justification than 'this is how I was raised' or 'this is just the way my family does it'. Instead, parenting decisions need to be based on what parents personally think to be in the best interests of their children.

Some parents end up subjecting their children to very damaging practices, ranging from neglect to violence and abuse. The effect of this is that some of the most vulnerable people in our society can be seriously harmed, physically and emotionally, or have their approach to life distorted. Rather than enjoying childhood, the children of such parents suffer until they manage to leave home — and sometimes for long after. From time to time society intervenes, removing children from their parents and placing them in the care of others, in institutions or in foster families. This is very much a case of the lesser evil since the evidence suggests that it is best to let children live with their parents whenever possible. The sad thing is that so-called bad parents rarely intend to harm their children: too often they are simply replicating what they experienced as children or are themselves suffering from a state of dysfunction and are unable to break the downward spiral that is enveloping their lives. They might indeed be bad parents, but this might be the best they can do.

To say that we should care for our children is not, however, to argue they must be protected from every risk or opportunity life offers. My own experience of childhood exposed me to some very risky environments. I would wander off to local bush areas and disappear for hours. I was able to play with 'bungers', including the notorious Thunderer, a powerful firework that could produce an impressive explosion. I learnt to drive old trucks, to ride (and fall off) horses, to plough a field with an old Fordson tractor—all before the age of fifteen. Yes, this was a different time. And I know that bungers are dangerous and that some children have lost fingers and eyes, leading to fireworks being banned in many places. But these risky behaviours were not only fun: they also helped me become adaptable and responsive.

Modern children face different demands and different risks. Allowing them to confront these obstacles can be frightening for parents, and doing so does not always work out well. My wife and I know this. The first time we allowed our son to go out on his own to a gathering of his mates, he ended up in hospital after being set upon by a gang of thugs. Fortunately, no lasting harm was done. It would have been easy for us to close down in a form of parental panic, but this was not the choice we made: instead, we accepted the risk that naturally comes with exposure to the world.

Another consideration concerns parents' desire to raise their children to be like them—in particular, to fit in with the social, cultural and religious conventions of the community to which the parents belong. Although this desire is understandable, in that parents often want their children to embrace and sustain their legacy, there are times when parents engage in practices that are best described as indoctrination. Rather than allowing their children to experience what they (the parents) are offering and then make up their own mind about the kind of life they want to live, some parents adopt (or allow others to adopt) techniques designed to limit their children's capacity to make autonomous choices.

At their most extreme, such parental interventions can extend to imposing physical changes on a child, as happens with male and female circumcision. Parents who institute or support such radical interventions believe they are doing so in the interests of their child—for example, to ensure that the child can fully belong to their community. But, as is proper, parental preferences are limited by the general standards that apply in the community they live in and are typically reflected in society's laws. That is why, in a country such as Australia, female circumcision, widely known as female genital mutilation, is prohibited.

The central test to be applied here is to do with the child's welfare. This test gives precedence to the idea that parents should expand— rather than restrict—a child's opportunities. In view of this, neglect, brutality, indoctrination and irreversible changes that limit, rather than augment, a child's capacity to make meaningful life choices are all considered illegitimate.

Finally, people occasionally ask whether there should be some sort of compulsory educative process designed to help prepare prospective parents for the challenges of raising children. The arguments against such a process typically involve an appeal to the value of liberty and a pragmatic realisation that there is no role for the state in overseeing, in a general sense, procreation. Nevertheless, a wider availability and use of voluntary educational programs, perhaps matched with incentives to participate, might do considerable good.

THE QUESTIONS

What are the boundaries within which parents should be permitted to raise their own children? How do we balance the parents' right to bring up children in their own (the parents') image against the right of a child to maintain the capacity to define their own life?

In particular:

×	Are you expanding or restricting your children's life opportunities?

×	Do you have a good grasp of the nature of the society in which your children will need to find their way?

×	What resources might you draw on to make yourself a better person (and parent) before having children and thereafter— family resources, the wisdom of your elders, and so on?

×	Are you unconsciously and uncritically replicating the practices of your own parents? Are those practices suitable?

×	Is your (quite natural) desire to protect your children from harm inappropriately restricting their life experience and their opportunities to learn how to manage risk and cope in the modern world?

×	Are you treating your children as people in their own right, or are you treating them as property or as smaller versions of yourself?

×	Where do you draw the boundary between acceptable and unacceptable parenting practices?

REFUGEES AND ASYLUM SEEKERS

For as long as there has been war, oppression, famine and pestilence there have been refugees and asylum seekers. Can we imagine the awfulness of waking up to find that the world we once knew has been overturned, with peace replaced by war, harmony blighted by perse-cution, and security shredded by fear? In circumstances like this, where death and destruction await those present, flight becomes an urgent need. Leaving behind memories, land, the resting places of ancestors, leaving behind almost everything of value, those who are forced to flee can also lose their identity, becoming part of a mass of humanity who, depending on their status, are either refugees or asylum seekers.[26]

Long ago the world developed the idea of sanctuary, or asylum. There is one core notion at work here—safety. To be clear, the offer of asylum or refuge does not involve a promise of happiness, prosperity or a new or better life: it simply involves recognition of the objective state of people fleeing for their lives and the offering of assistance and safety.

This is not to say that societies cannot, or should not, offer more. For example, some societies have established refugee intake programs that offer far more than simple safety. Among other things, they invest heavily in programs designed to help refugees make new lives in a new land. Such an investment can be prompted by compassion for the refugees, although the compassion can also be infused with a measure of self-interest—especially in view of the evidence that refugees often bring to their host society greater value than the cost of the society's investment in their integration.

---

26 A refugee is a person who has been granted protection by a government for one of the reasons stated in the 1951 Refugee Convention. An asylum seeker is someone seeking refuge or asylum but who has not yet been granted that protection.

The number of people being displaced from their homeland is increasing. Some people choose to seek out a more prosperous life away from their homeland, but the vast majority of people seeking refuge are forced to do so by cruel need. Many stop and stay at the first safe place they find, often remaining in refugee camps established in areas bordering intense conflict; there they might remain for decades, either awaiting an end to hostilities or hoping for resettlement through formal government and international programs. Others feel they should not or cannot wait, instead seeking to make their way by whatever means are available to the potential site of a new home.

It is this latter group that has caught the world's attention, causing a backlash from some politicians and policy makers who are determined to neither encourage nor support irregular patterns of arrival. The reasons for this opposition vary. Some policies are based on calculations of political self-interest: there are votes to be gained in being tough on strangers. There are, however, also a number of ethically important reasons for opposing the free flow of asylum seekers, among them fears for the health and safety of those who are open to exploitation by people smugglers, who take their fee regardless of whether their cargoes live or die; a fear that official refugee intakes will be reduced if voters feel their government has lost control of its borders; and concern that a disorderly system is unfair to those who play by the rules.

It is obviously a complex problem, and people of genuine compassion and goodwill can find themselves on different sides of the debate. The only way to resolve the differences of view is to go back to first principles. And this means looking again at the purpose of asylum, which is to offer safety (neither more nor less) to those whose circumstances have placed them in danger. This very basic standard then allows one to evaluate specific policies: at their heart, do they help people to be safe? Or do they expose people to new risks of harm? If the latter is the case, those policies fail the most basic test of validity.

Finally, it should be acknowledged that there is neither merit nor fault in being born in a particular place at a particular time. It is a matter of luck that some people are safe and some are at grave risk. As a result, the idea that our fate should be decided according to lines drawn on a map must be open to question. This could become an increasingly important consideration if climate change prompts mass migrations from rural and urban areas that are no longer viable as places of human habitation.

THE QUESTIONS

To what extent, if any, do we have an obligation to assist strangers who are in need of protection from genuine risks of death or persecution?

In particular:

× Can we use our imagination to place ourselves in the shoes of people whose lives are at risk through no fault of their own? Is there any good reason to treat those people differently from the way we would want to be treated in similar circumstances?

× Are the policies of different political parties and governments around the world both practical and principled?

× Is safety assured, which is the fundamental motivator of policy designed to provide asylum?

× Is this the kind of problem that can be resolved only through international cooperation? If so, is each country carrying a reasonable share of the burden?

⨯ Can we see behind slogans and headlines in order to understand the real reasons for particular policies and actions to anticipate some of the unintended consequences of taking one approach or another?

RELATIONSHIP BREAKDOWNS

Not all relationships endure. Despite the best intentions, people can grow apart. This might be caused by a life-changing event, by the discovery of some aspect of a person's character that had previously been unknown, or because a 'better offer' comes along.

The impact of a break-up grows in proportion to the time and depth of the commitment that existed before problems emerged. For example, a casual dalliance, or hooking up, might lead nowhere because neither person expected a commitment. Obviously, it becomes harder if a commitment has been made or assumed. Then there is the effect on others such as children. Because of this some people opt to stay together, not so much for their own sake but for the sake of others. They might even decide to continue living together while one party enters a new relationship, thus allowing each other a degree of freedom within the confines of a continuing commitment to preserving the basic family unit. This can be an acceptable solution if the costs to either partner are not too great. In cases of domestic violence, though, or if the underlying difficulties are producing profound unhappiness, this might not be an option.

It is almost never the case that both parties realise at the same time that their relationship needs to come to an end, so responsibility usually falls on just one of the partners to deal with the situation. Some people cannot bear to deliver news they know will devastate the other person and carry on as if nothing has happened, living a lie. Some people are not brave enough to confront the other person, so they disappear—sometimes literally, sometimes by withdrawing into themselves. And some people are both cowardly and callous, unable to look the other person in the eye, instead sending a text message or email.

For the most part, however, honesty and compassion are the best choice. It might be that the relationship can be repaired if the other person is made aware of the problem; after all, there must have been an original 'spark'. It might be that people just need time to work through the difficulties that are putting the relationship at risk. Or it might be that there is nothing more to be said or done, that it is time to move on—if possible, preserving friendship and respect where there once was love and passion.

The main thing is to cause as little harm as possible while being true to oneself. And that requires courage.

THE QUESTIONS

The end of a relationships is always messy. The temptation is to ignore what is happening, to avoid the unpleasantness. But if things have moved beyond the point of no return, how can the relationship be brought to an end with the least amount of harm to others?

In particular:

- ⨯ Are there shared expectations and understandings about the relationship? Was it always meant to be casual and temporary? Was it meant to be exclusive?

- ⨯ Is the relationship worth fighting for? Is there a possibility of recovery?

- Who will be affected if the relationship ends? How can their interests be protected?

- Is there room for compromise? Does the relationship have to be on an all-or-nothing basis? What modifications might work for both people—for example, sharing roles or spending more time together?

- What external factors might be at work? Can they be managed?

- How can the message be delivered with honesty and compassion?

RELIGIOUS AND CULTURAL RIGHTS

Australia is a rich and diverse society, bringing together people with differing views about what makes for a good life, for individuals and societies. Of course, not all these views are compatible. Indeed, religious beliefs are founded on 'exclusive-truth' claims about the nature of god (or the gods); that is, most religions claim that their view is the correct view and that others are in error. History shows us time and again that religious differences can lie behind war and multiple other types of abhorrent human behaviour. Yet, at its best, religion can also inspire some of humankind's greatest achievements—acts and works of vaulting imagination and the deepest compassion. Humanity has, however, not yet found a way of having all that is good in religion without the horrible.

Often bound up with, but separate from, religious differences are cultural questions. Culture precedes religion, which is itself a part of culture. Cultural differences can also give rise to conflict—especially when linked to other ways of deciding what is appropriate human behaviour. For example, some cultures allow men, and sometimes women, concurrently to have multiple sexual partners; some cultures express themselves through rituals that involve pain and bloodshed of a kind that others judge unacceptable. Although differences like this can be a source of general enrichment, they can also stir resentment — especially when people with culturally different views and practices are competing for the same, limited resources.

Western societies encountered all these problems before finding a solution to major forms of religious and cultural conflict during the European Enlightenment of the eighteenth century. The Enlightenment's primary innovation was to establish secular states in which the populace would be governed by the rule of law. A secular state is not one that is hostile to religion: rather, it is indifferent, neither privileging nor persecuting religious belief. All it requires is that every person, whatever their religion or culture, will obey laws made for the sake of all. Democracies in various forms have been the preferred form of government because they have been well suited to reconciling differences of opinion by peaceful means. One of the results of these innovative notions has been that people of differing, and sometimes competing, cultures and religions have been able to live together in relative harmony.

Secular liberal democracies did not emerge over night or fully formed: they have evolved over centuries, enlightened both by practice and by the work of a host of philosophers exploring aspects of politics, ethics and economics in particular.

From time to time groups claim that the laws of secular society are inconsistent with their religious beliefs and practices and that freedom of belief—something championed by most secular liberal democracies—must be unconstrained by the state. Most defenders of secular liberal democracies would agree that belief should be unconstrained. Some cultural and religious groups, however, seek something more than just freedom of belief: they want to be able to give effect to their beliefs by engaging in particular practices. For example, some cultural groups reserve the right to circumcise their children, even though others argue that this is a form of mutilation; and some religious groups exclude specific people from their institutions, such as people who do not share their beliefs or who have a lifestyle they condemn as immoral.

It is this translation of belief into practice that causes the greatest difficulty. The challenge for society then becomes one of balancing the rights of citizens in general against the rights of cultures or religions and their adherents. In general terms, secular societies are happy to allow cultural and religious practices to be applied to adults who freely choose to accept them or to children if the practice is neither fundamentally detrimental nor irreversible. There is thus a reluctance to accord cultural or religious practices a privileged place in society *in general* or to accept associated beliefs as sufficient reason for curbing the civil liberties of any person (even if that person happens to be a recognised member of a particular culture or faith group). That is, the state usually offers public protection against the imposition of private beliefs, using the law as the basis for determining what is appropriate. Because of this, some religious and cultural groups seek special exemptions from the application of the law, either in general or in particular contexts (such as within the precincts of their own organisations).

It must be acknowledged that few societies offer a 'level playing field' for all cultures and religions. For example, Australian life has been shaped by the Judeo–Christian tradition in ways that are more or less taken for granted. There is, however, a deeper problem for countries such as Australia. The Enlightenment solution might be suitable as a policy framework for dealing with religions and cultures that arrived after European settlement, but what of the earlier traditions of Aboriginal and Torres Strait Islander peoples? Their practices had been developed over millennia before Europeans arrived, so why should they be bound by the views of latecomers?

This latter question is of great importance, especially when it comes to the application of customary law. When the English wrested possession of what is now called Australia from its Indigenous inhabitants—by force when necessary—they imposed one system on many and forced into their control peoples that never consented to incorporation in a foreign state. This situation was radically different from that applying to all subsequent migrants to Australia, who have come knowing that they will be bound by Australian laws.

THE QUESTIONS

To what extent should a secular liberal democracy make allowance for its citizens to express their religious and cultural beliefs in everyday practice?

In particular:

- Should special allowance be made for the traditional cultural practices of Aboriginal and Torres Islander peoples?

- Should the expression of religious and cultural beliefs be limited to private places?

- Should Australia follow the example of a country such as France, which has sought to ban the display of religious symbols in state schools?

- Should the basic rights of citizens (such as the right to be protected from discrimination) apply in all cases—even in settings controlled by religious and cultural organisations?

REWARDING CHILDREN

Just as punishment might constrain a child's behaviour, so can the promise of a reward—at least in the short term. That might sound fairly innocent, and I have to confess to having bribed my children in the past. Of course, I could try to describe my behaviour by using a more acceptable term such as 'offering incentives'. But that would be to avoid the truth, which is that on occasion a well-placed bribe might seem to be the lesser evil when seeking a peaceful life. From memory, I never resorted to money—or is that selective memory?— although I do recall bribes involving food (ice-cream and burgers, say) and opportunities (usually to do something otherwise restricted).

There is something to be said for recognising and rewarding good behaviour. A kind word, a bonus or an unexpected ice-cream can go a long way in reinforcing good behaviour. Ideally, children eventually come to do good things for their own sake; in fact, it is important that they learn to do so—without the prospect of reward. As long as children are doing the right thing for the right reason there is nothing wrong with some external recognition and reward. The thing to avoid is children coming to believe that the main, or only, reason for doing good is reward.

As for what counts as a good reward, what we now know about the risks of things such as trans-fats and refined sugars should probably cause us to drop sweets and fast foods from the list of potential rewards. More often than not, recognition and a word of praise are all that is required. As for my own example, it seems that, instead of rewarding good behaviour, I was trying to prevent bad behaviour— and by questionable means.

THE QUESTIONS

How do we make sure children don't learn the wrong lessons—in particular, that they conclude we should do good deeds only when there will probably be a reward or other benefit of some kind?

In particular:

× Are you rewarding good behaviour or trying to prevent bad behaviour?

× Is the nature of your proposed reward appropriate—healthy, suited to the circumstances and so on?

× Can you be confident that your child will not draw the wrong conclusions from observing your behaviour?

× If you are not the child's parent, do you have the parents' permission to reward this child? Is your relationship with the child such that it is appropriate to take this course of action?

ROMANCE VERSUS CASUAL ENCOUNTERS

Some say it was Eleanor of Aquitaine who championed the idea of 'courtly love', a romantic ideal of unrequited, sex-free love, whereby knights would joust and woo in order to gain the favour of a noblewoman who would barely acknowledge their presence. It has also been suggested that this was simply Eleanor's ingenious way of controlling a castle full of testosterone-fuelled thugs (masquerading as knightly characters) keen to bed any woman they could. Perhaps this is too cynical; perhaps there was a genuine romantic ideal at play. Whatever the case, from then until now society has been marked by both romantic liaisons and casual encounters. In the case of the former, the whole person—mind, body and emotions—

is usually the focus of attention, and the challenge is to secure the affections of someone over time and in a form that might endure. In contrast, casual encounters are usually a product of nothing but lust, a physical attraction that has no purpose other than its own satisfaction.

Problems arise when the nature of these two types of relationship becomes confused, especially when one party is hoping for romance and the other is motivated by naked lust. Like most of the 'vices', lust is resistant to rational control, by either individuals or society, and tends to have been frowned on. Added to that is the practical concern that lust can too easily lead to unplanned pregnancies, not to mention sexually transmitted diseases. In earlier times unplanned pregnancies posed a threat to property, position and the orderly progression of society. No wonder rulers such as Eleanor of Aquitaine looked to the church to help them regulate lust—not just through the ideal of courtly love but also through the threat of punishment as the 'wages of sin'.

Modern societies concern themselves little with such questions of public order, especially since effective contraception is widely available. These days casual relationships between consenting adults pose far less risk to society; instead, the concern expressed about casual sex is more to do with personal morality and the idea that self-restraint, chastity, and so on, are characteristics to be prized for their own sake and as an indication of the character of the individual. It is against this background that romance can be considered preferable by some—because it takes time and an investment by both parties and involves the whole person and not just their basic urges.

THE QUESTIONS

This is ultimately a matter of personal choice. Do you choose to invest in the more challenging prospect of romance or do you choose simply to enjoy the satisfaction of casual sex—freely given, freely received and without any continuing obligation? For some, this might be sufficient—at least for the moment.

In particular:

× Do both parties have the same expectations? How do you know?

× Might there be unintended consequences—including lasting obligations that you have not considered?

× Are you exposing yourself to censure from people who might not seem to care but in reality are ready to condemn you for doing what they only pretend to support? This is a particular concern for women, who can face 'slut shaming', often from other women.

× Are you willing to bear the 'costs' of romance, in that you will expose more of yourself and therefore might find it harder to cope with rejection?

× Do you care about maintaining self-control? Is your concept of virtue—or that of those you most admire—reconcilable with how you propose to act?

SCHOOL FUNDING AND FEES

No person's child is more valuable than another person's, and our being born into a particular kind of family is a matter of pure accident. In view of this, should we not ensure that every child has access to education of the same quality?

Private schools have their place, especially when they are catering for people who want their child to be exposed to a specific ethos. In spite of this, though, no child should be diverted from the state system simply because a parent believes a private school will offer a better education. The challenge here is not to seek the closure of all private schools: it is to ensure that every state school has sufficient funding and resources so that, if there is a relative deficiency, the state's standards meet or exceed the best the private schools have to offer.

The decisions parents make about schools will necessarily reflect their personal circumstances, their knowledge of their child, and their aspirations for their child's progress in society. There is, however, also a wider social dimension to be taken into account when making such decisions and an obligation to ensure that the choice one makes for one's own child is not to the detriment of any other child. This is not to say we have obligations to other people's children. Rather, the point is to consider why, in the absence of any sound reason, the advantage of one should come at the expense of another.

There is also a larger consideration—to do with the potential costs to society of having children grow up in differing, and sometimes competing, education systems. Competition can be healthy, especially when it is genuinely open, but is society diminished by major divergences in the experience of children as they grow up?

Finally, it must be acknowledged that many parents who send their children to private schools make substantial sacrifices in order to do so. It might not be their intention, but these parents also take on some of the burden of funding education. In the absence of private schools, governments' education costs would soar.

THE QUESTIONS

Under what conditions should people be free to send their children to private schools? Can the public and private sectors co-exist in a way that is fair to all concerned? Does society suffer if its children are educated in different cohorts?

In particular:

× Does the purchasing power of parents who send their children to private schools confer an unfair advantage?

× How can students attending state schools enjoy the same educational advantages as those attending private schools?

× Are there good reasons—to do with ethos, religion, and so on—for your child to attend a private school? Are the potential advantages real?

× Do the parents of children at private schools carry too small, or too great, a burden when it comes to the overall cost of education?

× Would society be better off if private schools were banned? Conversely, would society be better off if all schools were privatised?

SCIENCE AND TECHNOLOGY

Although some people think 'ignorance is bliss', the pace and direction of change are such that people who know nothing of science and technology are likely to be swept along with little say in the direction of their lives. This has ever been the case: those who control knowledge ultimately control society. That is why over the ages various elites restricted access to education. For a time power resided with those who could master disciplines such as theology, law, rhetoric and languages. Since the time of the Renaissance, though, increasing authority has been attached to those able to master the various scientific disciplines and convert scientific knowledge into effective technologies. This has led to revolutions in human practices ranging from medicine to agriculture, warfare, architecture and design.

It would seem the effects of science and technology are going to become more profound and far-reaching. Advances such as artificial intelligence and robotics, gene editing, and the creation of 'synthetic life' will transform human society and, potentially, life on earth.

In view of this, why would one choose not to know at least something about science and technology? We might not all possess deep expertise — but to know nothing? People once discovered how to make their way in the world by learning Latin, or more recently English, so should we now be learning one of the languages for computer programming so that we are not entirely dependent on others?

This is not to suggest we need to understand science only and nothing else: it is equally important to learn about other ways of understanding the world. Indeed, people working in science should also aim to have broad horizons: in particular, they should develop 'ethical literacy' so as to ensure that the science and technology they deploy can be used responsibly and with restraint.

THE QUESTIONS

Are there some forms of knowledge every person should be acquainted with if they are to be capable of making informed decisions about their lives and the nature of the society they live in?

In particular:

- How much of your world is being shaped by science and technology?

- Can you maintain independence of judgment and action without at least a basic understanding of science and technology?

- Should the government facilitate the acquisition of this basic knowledge by every citizen, whatever their age?

- Can we each make good use of free resources for learning that can be found on the internet? Is universal access to this material a matter of digital justice?

SETTING A FAIR PRICE

At their best, markets are supposed to allow for a free exchange of value—often embodied in a range of goods and services— in which prices are set through a process of open negotiation. This ideal rests on the assumption that both buyer and seller have perfect information—not only about how others are setting prices for the same goods and services but also about the true nature of what is being offered for sale. The system further assumes that all parties are equally free to choose, that there is no force or fraud involved. If these ideal conditions are met, the theory goes that the agreed price is the same as the 'fair' price; that is, there is no independent standard of fairness to which one might appeal. The standard is what happens to be agreed by a fair process.

Well, that's the theory. The reality is often different. For example, we have all heard of powerful retailers putting a metaphorical gun to the head of their suppliers, insisting on prices that producers know to be unsustainable. The effect is occasionally magnified in politically charged campaigns, which usually relate to the treatment of asset-rich but cash-poor farmers. (People seem to care less about small manufacturers, shopkeepers, and so on, who might be both asset-poor and cash-poor, but why that is so is another topic altogether.)

This idea also extends to negotiations on wages and conditions for employees. One of the reasons for the emergence of the union movement was to try to provide equal 'weight' for employees when negotiating with large companies. Whether or not individual employees are equal to companies—especially in times of high unemployment, and especially if there is minimal social security to fall back on—remains an open question.

THE QUESTIONS

The pressure big business applies to its smaller relations is often said to be justified in the name of getting a better deal for consumers.

If this were true would you be comfortable being complicit in a process that sets prices in conditions that are far short of the ideal?

In particular:

× To what extent do you benefit from prices that are set in conditions where the bargaining does not take place among equals? Is this acceptable to you?

× Have you ever been in an unequal bargaining position? How did it feel?

× Are there minimum requirements—such as the ability to recover costs or the capacity to maintain a dignified way of life—that should be taken into account when prices are set?

SEX

One overriding principle should be upheld when it comes to sex: it must be consensual. This principle applies regardless of the gender, identity or sexual orientation of the people involved, and it applies to every kind of sex, from the most straight-laced to the most exotic.

The requirement for consent does not simply involve a one-off agreement that can be presumed to be binding thereafter. Any person should be able to say no to sex at any time and have their wishes respected. This is despite the fact that until relatively recently in many Western societies a married woman was assumed to be unable to refuse to have sex with her husband. As a consequence, the concept of marital rape was largely unknown in the law until the latter part of the twentieth century. These older laws reflected what continues to be the view held in some other religions—that a wife may never, or only rarely, refuse to have sex with her husband.

There is, however, another side to these cultural norms. Some religions—Judaism comes to mind—place an obligation on both parties to ensure the sexual satisfaction of the other. Under such a code, one might be able to refuse to accept sex but not refuse to offer it to a partner.

Beyond the application of the primary principle—free and informed consent—there is much room for debate. Should sex be reserved for those who are married to each other? Is it to be associated only with the procreation of children? Is it just for fun? Can it be enjoyed with strangers? The list is long.

In any event, what arouses people seems to be mind-bendingly varied. I knew a taxi driver, a former British fighter pilot, who worked at night driving women to and from the brothel they worked in. He told me of a man whose predilection was to watch a woman stepping on snails while wearing a raincoat in the shower! 'Unpacking' that one is beyond the scope of this book.

The primary principle of requiring consent does, however, deal with most of the extreme cases. It explains, for example, why we should oppose sex involving children or other vulnerable people who cannot consent in the full and proper sense to sexual activity. As for the rest, what one thinks will depend on one's ethical framework.

THE QUESTIONS

Do people have an ongoing right to give or withhold their consent to sex? Is sex something that is fulfilling for those involved and consistent with respect for each person's intrinsic dignity?

In particular:

- ⨯ Is everyone genuinely comfortable with what is being proposed or is going on?

- ⨯ Is everyone safe and equally empowered to say yes or no?

- ⨯ Is anyone at risk of being used simply as an object for the satisfaction of others, with no regard for their dignity?

SEX AND GENDER

The differences between males and females are essential to the reproduction of species and the evolution of most, but not all, forms of life on earth. In nature, the sex of a creature will determine the role the creature plays, governing patterns of behaviour such as control of territory, courting rituals, care and feeding of offspring, hunting, and construction of habitats. There is, however, no fixed pattern for determining the particular role of sex in the natural world: sometimes males are the smaller of the two sexes; sometimes power is invested in females; sometimes males care for offspring. For every apparent rule there is an exception.

Although humans are biologically part of the animal kingdom, our capacity to make conscious choices allows us to loosen the bonds of nature and arrange the relationship between the sexes as we see fit.

At this point it is worth noting the distinction between a person's sex (for example, male or female) and their gender (for example, man or woman). The former is a matter of nature; the latter is a matter of construction through mechanisms such as socialisation.

As a result, there is as much variety in human societies as there is in the natural world. The only fixed thing is that it is women alone who can bear children. This biological fact has shaped some but not all societies. For example, males tend to fight wars and engage in more hazardous work not so much because they are naturally stronger or more aggressive but because it takes only one male to repopulate a community. If males were to stay safe and, say, only one woman returned from a battle, the community would be doomed. In that sense it is redundancy, from a population viewpoint, that makes men expendable.

Natural differences between men and women have also been reinforced by cultural patterns, which in turn are often influenced by religious beliefs. For example, in ancient times women often dominated rites associated with fertility and men were sacrificed to Mother Earth. Men later turned the tables by promoting the rival sky gods (for example, the Olympians led by Zeus). To this day, some Christians say women can never assume leadership of institutions, including families, because Christ was male. They argue that men and women are to perform roles that are 'equal but different'— an argument that gives scant satisfaction to those in the 'equal but subservient' roles, where merit counts for nothing.

Modern societies have escaped most of the limitations imposed by nature. This allows males and females to recalibrate the allocation of tasks so that members of each sex can perform roles that best allow them to flourish. Males can, in principle, be as nurturing as females; females can be as competitive as males. Variations within a sex can be as great as those between sexes and, in any case, modern machines tend to iron out the differences. These days it is possible for all roles, other than that of childbirth, to be swapped and shared between the sexes.

Yet women still perform the majority of household tasks—for no reason other than that this is a cultural hangover from times when assumptions about the respective capacities of males and females tended to locate women in the domestic zone and send men out into the world. Women naturally want to enjoy all the opportunities traditionally available to men. They know they can do the jobs men do with equal capacity and, as a matter of justice and personal fulfilment, demand to be allowed to do so. But many women are taking on these jobs while simultaneously performing the biologically necessary tasks of motherhood, in effect doubling their load.

Men might be slowly adjusting, taking on a fairer share of the work traditionally done by women in the home. Additionally, new labour-saving technologies and the emergence (and re-emergence) of domestic services such as child care and cleaning can allow for a more equitable distribution of the loads borne by women and men.

Finally, it is becoming clear that human gender is no longer a simple binary choice, if ever it was. Similar levels of variability are also to be found in relation to sex. Some people are born knowing their true gender is not in alignment with their apparent sex—for example, biological males who know they are women. Some people reject being identified as of any gender. It can seem hard to believe that biological markers of sex can be overridden by other factors until you meet a transgender person. Then all doubt is removed. Just as people who are homosexual have no choice in the matter—they are born as they are, part of the great diversity of nature—so it is with transgender people.

Of course, each of us has a choice in what to do about the given facts of our identity, but if being true to our identity causes no harm to others why would we not make this choice?

THE QUESTIONS

For most people, female or male gender is a given. The differences between the genders have become integral to cultural patterns. Now, though, we have the chance to reorder those patterns so as to afford individuals greater freedom to realise their own aspirations. Are there any reasons for not breaking religious, cultural and other conventions in the interest of equal opportunity?

In particular:

- Has the modern world liberated us from gender patterns emanating from nature?

- Is the allocation of tasks between men and women fair? Is it based on merit and competence or just age-old patterns?

- Does society give equal status to the roles traditionally played by women as opposed to those played by men? Will the situation change as more men take on the traditionally female roles?

- Apart from childbirth, are there any roles that cannot be shared between men and women?

- What might happen when technology allows a child to be nurtured in and born from an artificial womb?

- Can technology help us recalibrate expectations of gender?

- Does gender still matter—especially given the complexity of relationships and identities occurring naturally in the human population?

CONSCIENCE

We should act only according to a well-informed
(and well-formed) conscience.

SHARING ACCOMMODATION

In modern Western societies, people tend to live in small groups—in family homes, in apartments with friends and lovers and, in old age, with extended families or with other residents of aged-care facilities. In all cases the lines between private and common areas are blurred. For example, families typically share kitchens, sitting rooms, bathrooms and laundries. Bedrooms might be considered private, especially as children grow older, but no room is entirely 'private' in a family home. Rather, each forms part of a whole, where odours intermingle, noise travels down hallways, and junk and general mess can spread to the point where it cannot be concealed.

Residents who have the greatest impact rarely intend to cause difficulty. Typically, they treat their private space as a kind of refuge, where they can safely relax and be themselves. It does not occur to them that others might be having to pay a price, through extra work or stress, for the sake of their comfort.

THE QUESTIONS

We all need our privacy—a place to unwind and be ourselves. But what if our personal needs are incompatible with the needs of others with whom we share accommodation? What is a reasonable basis for compromise as an alternative to a breakdown in living arrangements?

In particular:

× Are you doing your fair share of the work to maintain the household? If not, who has taken on the additional burden? Do they do so willingly? Have they given you permission to do less than your fair share? Do you compensate in other ways?

- Is your private space genuinely yours? Or does your use of that space affect others? If others are exposed to your space, do you maintain a standard that is minimally acceptable to all?

- Are you aware of how your personal habits affect others? Is there room for adjustment or compromise?

- Are others compromising to meet your requirements? Should you reciprocate?

SHARING COSTS WHEN SOCIALISING

It is an Australian tradition to 'shout' your mates, usually when at the pub. In short, to shout is to buy something for others, usually with the expectation that the gesture be will reciprocated. Allow enough time and everyone in the group will hear the phrase, 'Your shout, mate.'

In view of the expectation of reciprocity, it is considered unethical to accept a shout but then avoid responsibility when it is your turn. Examples of this behaviour are claiming, 'I forgot to bring my wallet' or 'I'll get a double round next time'. It is still worse when someone 'discounts the shout' by substituting a cheaper option or by reducing the quantities—even if this might actually be the responsible thing to do.

The same situation can arise in a restaurant when everyone agrees to 'split the bill' and then one of the group consumes far more than anyone else. Equally irritating can be a person who tries to allocate every cent to every person on a user-pays basis.

In each case the common factors are fairness in general and reciprocity in particular. If you are out with friends who trust you enough to include you in a shout or to split a bill, what does it say about your character if you avoid paying for your share, even if the people you are with say they forgive you? If this behaviour becomes a pattern, you can quickly lose friends.

THE QUESTIONS

Much of life is governed by conventions rather than rules. Although not formally enforced, conventions help regulate social relations, and one of the most important aspects of social life is eating and drinking together. What should we do if the conventions are flouted by one of our number?

In particular:

- Did you agree to be part of the group, or were you just roped into the shout? Could you have extracted yourself without causing offence?

- Are you paying your fair share of the costs, or are you finding ways to pass your share on to others?

- What will people deduce about your character if you act unfairly? Does the opinion of people in the group matter to you?

- Are you bound by deeper obligations, such as those of friendship?

- How do you deal with a person who makes a habit of dodging their obligation? Do they have other qualities that compensate for this? Or do they have a genuine excuse, one they would not want to disclose to others, even friends?

- Were the rules for managing and allocating costs agreed at the outset?

'SICKIES'

Australian workers are relatively fortunate when it comes to the amount of paid holidays and leave they can enjoy. The standard four weeks' annual leave is at least double that available to employees in the United States. In addition, there are many public holidays and there are provisions for special types of leave, most importantly sick leave. Each type of leave is an employee entitlement and is activated by specific triggers. Annual leave is tied to time worked, for example, and compassionate leave is linked to tragic events such as a death in the family. Sick leave is triggered by illness. At least that's the theory.

In practice, there is also a form of leave known as the 'sickie', which refers to time taken off work while claiming to be unwell. Not surprisingly, sickies tend to occur most often on Mondays and Fridays or just before and after school holidays, enabling the enjoyment of a string of unofficial long weekends and extended holidays.

The fact that the word 'sickie' has become an ordinary part of our lexicon tells us much about the sickie's status in Australia. It seems to be commonplace, even though, on the face of it, it is a product of dishonesty. The whole idea of a sickie is to engage in deception while continuing to enjoy the rewards of employment. This is enabled by the fact that to date relatively few employers, outside of the public service, have required any objective evidence of illness. Sick leave largely operates on an honour system in which employees are trusted not to abuse the benefits that come from being paid while not at work. Considering that most people are honest and would never steal money or goods from their employer, why do so many steal time?

One explanation is that people approach sick leave on a use-it-or-lose-it basis. They think that, since the entitlement exists, their employer obviously has the capacity to cover the time and cost associated with people being away from work because of illness. The logic seems to be that the good fortune of being healthy should not be offset by the bad fortune of missing out on additional leave. A secondary factor seems to be the perception that everyone does it; that is, people feel it can't be so bad if so many other people do it, and the opportunity cost of being virtuous is too high. Finally, some set a fairly low bar when deciding when they are sick — where anything other than perfect health can be reason enough to stay at home.

The other side of the coin is illustrated by the person who goes to work when unwell. This defeats one of the purposes of sick leave — to try to prevent the healthy being infected by the unhealthy. An employer is done no favour by an employee who turns up at work only to end up sending the majority of the workforce to their beds.

Ideally, employment is a bargain made between employers and employees. In return for their effort, skills and diligence, employees receive a variety of benefits. The system depends on them to create at least enough income to fund their own remuneration. In turn, this depends on everyone contributing their fair share. Sickies, and other forms of unjustified leave, don't just have an adverse effect on employers: the greatest burden falls on other employees who have to make the extra effort to complete the work that funds the entire enterprise.

THE QUESTIONS

Is it right to take a sickie?

In particular:

- Would you be embarrassed if your employer or a colleague knew exactly what was going on when you took a sickie?

- Who is bearing the cost of your absence?

- Do you consider what you are doing to be dishonest? If so, what makes dishonesty acceptable in this case?

- Is your employer fair in their dealings with you? Does this give rise to a reciprocal obligation for you?

- If your leave is for a legitimate purpose, might it have been granted in any case if you had asked?

SOCIAL JUSTICE

Ernest Hemingway's son said his father once told him, 'You make your own luck.'[27] The sentiment behind this is easy to understand: that our fortune and circumstances are a product of our own efforts. Indeed, the idea has been behind a number of social and political movements that have focused on providing equality of opportunity rather than equality of outcome. The idea is intuitively appealing: if everybody is able to start the race of life from the same position, the results will largely be a product of individual skill and effort and the rewards will be allocated accordingly.

---

27 Speaking to his son Gregory, as quoted in Hemingway, G H (1976), *Papa, a Personal Memoir*, MW Books, New York—'You make your own luck, Gig. You know what makes a good loser? Practice.'

In reality, though, it is almost impossible to create a genuinely level playing field. For some groups, historical disadvantage might have left deep scars that limit individual opportunity. In addition, fortune (good or ill) does not lose its influence once the race has started. Plenty of diligent people, applying their skills to the best of their ability, can find themselves knocked sideways by events over which they have no control. It might be an illness, an accident or suicide; they might become collateral damage as a result of the folly of others; or they might be a victim of the impact of a natural disaster. People affected in ways such as these cannot be said to have deserved what has befallen them. And the effect of such events can be devastating—people losing their jobs, their homes, their lives.

Communities can, and do, come together to help offset the damage. But, although this can happen at the local level, not everyone has family or community members who can stop them from falling through the cracks. That is where governments need to step in, marshalling public resources to support those in need. The downside of a compassionate response can, however, be that some people become dependent on welfare, and the dependence can spread from generation to generation, stifling the urge to be self-reliant and to contribute to the welfare of society. Dependency can also breed resentment and us-and-them rifts in the community.

THE QUESTIONS

How do we make adequate provision for the welfare of people who, through no fault of their own, find themselves in need of assistance? Can this be done without creating dependence? What is the right balance between compassion and the principle of self-reliance and freedom in the community?

In particular:

× How would you feel if you were in need of help and no one in your family or community was willing to assist?

× Should everyone receiving government support be required to contribute to their own welfare—for example, by doing a minimum amount of paid work? Should there be exceptions when a person is genuinely unable to make a contribution?

× What is the best way to get people back on their feet? Should society set limits on its support? Should society condemn those who appear able but are unwilling to make their own luck? Is encouragement to be preferred? Might the best response be a mix of these approaches?

× Does society really offer equality of opportunity or is this just a myth?

× Does society have an obligation to create opportunities such as training and jobs for people so that they can become independent?

SOCIAL MEDIA: FOR GOOD AND ILL

In the mid-2000s US company AOL commissioned and distributed two advertisements aimed at starting a discussion about whether the internet is a good or a bad thing. The two ads featured the same actor, John Hurt, providing the narration. The combination of Hurt's voice, the script and a deft choice of images allowed AOL to present two radically different views about what the internet might become.

In the time since the ads were made the internet has revealed itself to be a huge force for good. It has, however, also been used to unleash and amplify many of the most base and degrading aspects of human nature. On both counts social media have played a central role. The promise of social media was that they would liberate millions by allowing for direct, uncensored connection between friends, acquaintances and the general public, and for many this promise has been realised. But the same technologies have been used to cause others to suffer in ways unimaginable just a couple of decades ago. This is because the technologies' strengths—among them anonymity and 'reach'—can, like those of any technology, be used or abused.

The ability to present ideas, evidence and arguments to a large group of people has been of immense benefit to those wishing to call attention to the wrongdoing of the powerful. Most important has been the cover of anonymity—especially when criticising regimes with the will and capacity to punish detractors. Yet the very factors that might embolden a person to criticise the powerful can also be used to attack the weak.

In recent years there have been repeated instances of people being targeted by cyber-bullies. The attacks can be direct (the victim is made aware) or indirect (rumour, innuendo, and so on, circling the target without their knowing). And the harm can range from verbal insults and untruths to the use of degrading and violent images. The basis for such attacks can be revenge, cruelty, even punishment for not conforming to a dominant group's norms. In all cases, though, the intention is to hurt by means such as exclusion and humiliation. Bullying of this kind might not involve blows, but it has physical and psychological effects that undermine the dictum that 'sticks and stones may break my bones but words will never hurt me'.

How has this come about? The first thing to note is that people in general—and young people in particular—tend to underestimate the significance of what they do online when creating and distributing content. For example, the practice of sexting (sending intimate images to a lover or friend) can leave behind a near-permanent record. All that is needed is for the lover or friend to be untrustworthy and the image can be circulated in an instant. An image that might have been a token of love or affection can just as easily be used as a weapon. If a relationship ends in recriminations or some rogue element gains access to the image the damage can quickly be done.

It is not only images that can do harm. So can misplaced words—secrets shared, vulnerabilities revealed. The first thing people need to consider is whether their online presence is exposing them to risk. It is relatively easy to prevent potentially dangerous material from being created in the first place, certainly when compared with trying to manage a damaging leak.

The larger question concerns what happens to patterns of ethical restraint when people enter the online world, especially under the cover of anonymity. People can say and do things online that they would never contemplate face to face with the person concerned. Live contact with someone exposes us to the full force of their response. If we are cruel we cannot escape their hurt; if we are rude and unfair we must count on their rebuke. We have to live with the consequences of what we do. None of this is a factor when we use remote digital means.

Of course, the lack of external restraint does not necessarily mean we must cut loose. Self-control is always a possibility. So is the effect of moral imagination, in which we put ourselves in the shoes of the other person. It takes some effort to move beyond one's own personal perspective, but it is possible. Use of moral imagination not only protects the potential victim; it can also protect a potential perpetrator from the remorse that often comes to bullies who have been exposed.

As the internet evolves we are becoming better at regulating its dark side. In part, this has grown out of our recognition of its power, especially to multiply effects, even to the extent that complete strangers become part of one's life.

One particular risk has been greatly increased by the development of the internet, and that is the risk to the integrity of one's identity. Digital fingerprints can be indelible, so if someone steals our identity whatever they do can be permanently linked to us. They might spend our money or seize our opportunities but, worst of all, they might destroy our good name. Hence the importance of digital security—strong passwords, encryption, and so on. A little effort in maintaining privacy and security can prevent a world of hurt.

Finally, there is the question of whether or not a person should be required to acknowledge that they are wearing a digital mask— that is, pretending to be someone they are not. This is a matter of balance between the occasional need for anonymity and the right not to be deceived. In times past this would have been achieved by a person actually wearing a mask, which would protect their identity but also alert others to the possibility of deception. It might be time to consider something similar for users of the internet. Are there means of digital identification available so that, although I might not know another person's identity, I can know that they are not who they are purporting to be?

THE QUESTIONS

Digital technology offers individuals and society a powerful means of doing good and doing ill. How might we make use of this technology without causing harm to others?

In particular:

- Are you revealing too much of yourself? Might you live to regret your online decisions?

- To what extent do you have genuine control over your digital presence?

- Are you taking sufficient care with your personal online security?

- Do you behave online in the way you would if face to face with the people potentially affected by your conduct?

- Do you have the consent of others to use their digital material—especially if it is provided in conditions of trust?

- Have you thoroughly assessed the harm or good you might do online—especially in view of the technology's capacity to amplify effects?

- Do you use anonymity responsibly?

- Are you comfortable with others knowing you are wearing a digital mask?

SPEAKING OUT ABOUT WRONGDOING

Much of the evil that has been done in the world could have been prevented if people had been willing to speak out. The most egregious examples are associated with events such as the rise of

Nazism and the genocide that formed part of the persecution of Europe's Jewish people. Time and again the historical record shows people watching in silence as the embers caught alight. Was it fear? Disbelief? Approval? All we know is that if enough people had objected the Holocaust might have been prevented.

On a less grotesque level, I was once asked to look into an incident in a corporation where an employee had stolen 20 million dollars (yes, *20 million*). It turned out that the employee's colleagues had known what was happening and had said nothing. The manager used this as an excuse—that he had not been told. It didn't occur to the manager to ask how it could be that he had presided over a workplace in which at least some people thought it best to say nothing about such a theft. He could not conceive of the possibility that he might have had a hand in creating or condoning a culture in which theft was not only possible but had actually happened.

On hearing about Singapore's capitulation to the Japanese in World War 2 and having learnt of the lack of British preparedness for a Japanese attack from the Malay Peninsula, Prime Minister Winston Churchill is said to have told the House of Commons, 'I did not know. I was not told. I should have asked.'[28] Plenty of modern leaders shelter behind the first two of Churchill's statements. Relatively few admit to the third, preferring to live in a state of 'plausible deniability'.

When leadership sinks to this level of irresponsibility, it makes it especially difficult for people to express their concerns. And even when formal mechanisms exist to protect people who report suspected wrongdoing—whistleblower protection, for example—

28 *Sydney Morning Herald* (2003), 'Leaders still myopically in thrall to sultans of spin', http://www.smh.com.au/articles/2003/07/11/1057783358957.html.

people who do speak out typically fare poorly. It can take a great deal of courage to put your head above the parapet.

Very few of us are bound by a formal obligation to 'speak truth to power' or to unmask the wicked. There are hazards in doing so—for reputation, for personal prosperity, even for life and limb. Yet to remain silent is to risk becoming complicit in the perpetration of avoidable evil.

THE QUESTIONS

We all know that people who seek to do ill prefer the shadows. Yet we also know that just one word from us might be enough to raise the shutters and expose wrongdoing. How do we balance personal welfare with the possibility of increasing the welfare of many?

In particular:

- Can the wrongdoing be exposed without your becoming directly involved? Is anonymity a possibility?

- Is the good you might do in speaking out too little to justify the personal cost resulting from disclosure?

- Can existing mechanisms offering protection be trusted to work?

- Will you be able to live with yourself if you say nothing?

- How would you feel if someone you love was the victim of wrongdoing that might have been prevented if only someone (or even you) had spoken up?

- Do you have allies who might join you, thus allowing for presentation of a united front?

SURROGACY

Some women are unable to conceive and bear children, a situation that can arise for a variety of reasons. There might come a time when there is a technological solution to this problem—where an external artificial womb will be available to allow a child to be conceived and grown outside a human body. For now, though, the only option for some aspiring parents is to find a woman who is prepared to be a surrogate mother during the pregnancy.

In Australia the law gives a birth mother primary (overriding) rights in relation to any child to whom she gives birth. This remains the case despite the content of written agreements (contracts) and even if the newly born child is genetically unrelated to the birth mother. It is therefore essential that there be a relationship of strong trust between the surrogate and the people who hope to raise the child as their own. Current Australian law does not allow for commercial surrogacy, whereby a woman is paid to carry a child. Instead, Australian law recognises only altruistic surrogacy and allows for the surrogate to be compensated by the intended parents for reasonable costs incurred in the course of the pregnancy; this usually includes the opportunity cost of lost wages.

Ethical concerns generally present themselves when people seek out commercial surrogacy services in overseas countries, among them concerns about the extent to which the women offering surrogacy services are genuinely free to do so, the extent to which the surrogate mother receives just remuneration (as opposed to middlemen taking the larger part), and the difficulties that can arise in a foreign jurisdiction if something goes wrong with the health of the surrogate or the child, or in the relationship between the surrogate and the intended parents.

THE QUESTIONS

Has the surrogate mother previously given her free and informed consent to carry the intended parents' child? Is the understanding between the surrogate mother and the intended parents based on trust rather than mere contractual obligation?

In particular:

× Ethical obligations fall on all parties—including the surrogate mother. Do all parties have a common understanding of their respective rights and responsibilities?

× Do you understand the full chain of responsibility? For example, is the surrogate mother acting alone or with adequate support? Is she making her own decisions?

× How will matters be decided if complications arise during pregnancy?

× Have you considered what will be done if the child is born unwell or with a birth defect?

× Is the compensation just?

× What boundaries, if any, will be set now and for the future for the relationship between the intended parents, the surrogate mother and the child?

SUSTAINABILITY

Human ingenuity and the desire for increased prosperity have seen our species exploit the planet's natural resources to the point where we now consume more than the earth can replenish. Until now we have benefited greatly from this state of affairs; for example, in recent years there has been a sharp decline in global poverty, even though the affluent have been consuming ever more. Sooner or later, however, the imbalance will turn to the detriment of humanity. The beginnings of this can already be seen in the form of global warming, which heralds a catastrophic rise in sea levels, mass displacement of human populations, the collapse of large areas used for food production, and a concomitant threat to the peace and stability on which civilisation depends.

But this is not inevitable. Humans are smart—smart enough to be able to make different choices. Some of these choices will create new forms of wealth and prosperity; some will be based on our species' remarkable capacity to harness our intellect, through science and technology, in order to create solutions.

This depends, however, on there being a will to change, to invest in a different future. Whether or not we make this change depends on how one counts the personal cost of opting for sustainability and the extent of each person's 'circle of concern'. Who counts as important—just oneself, one's immediate family, the nation, the world, future generations? These and similar questions should also be considered by 'non-natural' persons such as corporations and institutions within the public and private sectors.

THE QUESTIONS

Human beings are consuming natural resources at a rate that is unsustainable. The costs of our doing so are already becoming apparent. We have the capacity to change, but do we have the will?

In particular:

× How should the costs and benefits of change be distributed? Should the more affluent be required to bear a greater burden, even if they are at little personal risk when compared to others?

× What are the most efficient and effective means for achieving sustainability?

× Is the challenge of sustainability a technical problem that can be resolved with human ingenuity? Or is it a human problem that can only be resolved by a change in attitudes and beliefs?

× What steps would we refuse to take—on ethical grounds—even if they might work to humanity's and the planet's advantage? For example, would we countenance population control? Would we ban specific goods and services?

× Are political systems based on democracy and personal liberty able to respond adequately to challenges such as global warming? Or is the market a better alternative? Is there an alternative system that would be better equipped to meet the challenges before us?

TAX MINIMISATION

The great American revolutionary, legislator and scientist Benjamin Franklin is credited with the maxim, 'In this world nothing can be said to be certain except death and taxes.'[29] More recently, a not-so-illustrious person, an Australian businessman, called into question the certainty of Franklin's claim when he told a parliamentary inquiry, 'Anybody in this country who does not minimise his tax wants his head read.'[30]

The evidence of recent years would suggest that plenty of people—especially rich and powerful individuals and corporations—have taken the businessman's advice to heart. Official investigations and the publication of leaked documents have made public a web of institutional arrangements that can be used to minimise tax, to the extent that not a cent is paid. One corporate heavy who actively sought to minimise the tax he paid told me that because he employed many people—all of whom paid their fair share of tax—he felt he had already 'done his bit' for the country.

Of course, it is not just some of the wealthy and powerful who are inclined to pay as little tax as possible. There is a thriving cash economy in which 'discounts' can be secured on the basis that unpaid tax represents a saving to be split between supplier and purchaser. It is never put as crudely as that; instead, those involved turn a blind eye and pocket the revenue. For most of us, though, there is not much opportunity to minimise tax: it is automatically deducted from our pay and sent to the tax office.

---

29 Originally in a letter from Franklin to Jean-Baptiste Leroy, 1789, which was reprinted in *The Works of Benjamin Franklin* (1817). See http://www.phrases.org.uk/meanings/death-and-taxes.html .

30 Kerry Packer said this in evidence given to a 1991 parliamentary inquiry, variously quoted, http://www.smh.com.au/federal-politics/political-news/corporate-tax-inquiry-kerry-packers-infamous-committee-appearance-serves-as-a-cautionary-tale-20150408-1mgfaq.html.

The obvious problem is that taxes are needed to fund the government services citizens rely on—defence, diplomacy, the courts, hospitals, schools, police, roads and bridges, and so on. Even if you are a fan of small government and think most things should be left to the private sector, any modern government needs a certain amount of money if it is to be able to function, and that money comes from taxes.

The problem with tax minimisation by individuals and corporations is that the funds forgone are simply transferred as costs to those who are willing to pay. Hence the 'free rider'—someone willing to accept the benefits of government without making a fair contribution to the costs. Think of a person who goes to a pub and accepts drinks from their mates without ever 'shouting' the group or of a person who goes to a restaurant but doesn't pay their fair share of the bill.

There are rules to do with taxation, and they allow people to make lawful deductions. Where there are rules, however, there are also potential loopholes. These are the plaything of lawyers and accountants. If you can afford the services of these professionals, you might be able to take advantage of some sloppy drafting and benefit from another person's error for what are almost certainly entirely selfish reasons. That then becomes the ethical test: when it comes to tax do we apply the spirit of the law or just the letter?

THE QUESTIONS

Most people want the benefits that accrue from the government's provision of services, but those services come at a cost. If we sometimes have a choice about how much tax we pay, should we pay what we reasonably believe to be owed or do we seek to minimise the amount?

In particular:

- If we don't pay our fair share of tax who will?

- Is it fair that we pay the tax that is due but that individuals and corporations with the resources to minimise their tax pay less? Does their behaviour alter the nature of our own obligation?

- Should the amount of tax paid be related to the quantity of government services used—more of a user-pays system? Or are there core government services (such as defence) that all taxpayers should support?

- Should everyone pay something—even welfare recipients?

- Do your perceptions about government waste or the efficient use of your taxes influence your decisions?

- Is the likelihood of getting caught a deterrent when it comes to tax minimisation?

- Is paying tax—like turning up to vote—one of the basic obligations of citizenship?

TEACHING RELIGION IN SCHOOLS

Modern Australia is a secular liberal democracy, a product of the European Enlightenment of the eighteenth century. The full range of cultural inputs—including a Judeo–Christian world view—has shaped the nation's culture and institutions. As a secular state, however, the Commonwealth of Australia is committed to the general propositions that there be freedom of belief and that religions and their adherents be neither persecuted nor advantaged.

The Europeans who first came to Australia did not take such an enlightened view. The colonising power had an established religion, the Church of England, and was at best dismissive of Roman Catholicism, which was not only the religion of a large number of the settlers but also the founding Christian denomination from which the Church of England had emerged. The result was that two 'warring camps' disembarked in Sydney Cove. Apart from dispossessing the local inhabitants, the Europeans also sought to carve out spiritual and temporal territory.

For a short time the churches controlled the schools, using educational institutions as one of their means of collecting and holding souls for whichever version of the Christian God they supported. The result was a patchwork of parochial schools that educated some, but certainly not all, of the colony's children. In New South Wales this eventually led people such as explorer and politician William Wentworth and Henry Parkes, a self-made man who attributed his success to a decent education, to propose and then introduce state-run education. Thus ended the churches' monopoly. They protested and eventually won a concession that gave them the right to teach scripture in New South Wales state schools for up to an hour a week. Until recently this was pretty much the case for all of Australia. The exception is the State of Victoria, where scripture may no longer be taught as a discrete subject; instead, all children are to be introduced to aspects of general or comparative religion.

Some people, such as those who advocated the removal of scripture teaching from Victorian schools, argue that a secular state should not allow religions to proselytise in its institutions. This is a general argument and is not related to the character or quality of the material being taught. Others have specific complaints relating to precisely what is being taught; for example, one of my children returned from school and reported that in scripture they had been taught that 'all the Jews are going to hell'. Not just some—the whole lot!

One of the best ways to build strong community bonds is for all children to experience a shared, public education, at least in primary school. Given this, one of the strongest arguments for allowing scripture teaching in secular state schools is that it might encourage religious parents to send their children there. Whether or not the availability of scripture in these settings has this effect is an empirical question. In principle, a weekly period of properly regulated scripture might be a price worth paying so that all communities are comfortable enough to have their children attend. The main requirement is that the material be *suitable*—and not the kind of rubbish taught to my children. This is a responsibility that falls on any state that opens its schools to any group, religious or otherwise.

Finally, governments need to maintain a principled commitment to being even-handed when dealing with all the groups offering classes to children in schools. Regrettably, some governments need to deal with politicians who not only control the balance of power but also wear their religion on their sleeve. It is here, in the lobbies where political deals are done, that the secular ideal of religious neutrality can be whittled away.

THE QUESTIONS

Should a secular liberal democratic state allow religious groups to teach their faith using state school facilities during the school day?

In particular:

- Does the state have sufficient oversight of what is being taught so as to ensure that the material is appropriate?

- Is the basic idea of a state school facilitating religious instruction improper?

- Would education in comparative religion be a better option than specific lessons in scripture?

- Does the availability of scripture teaching have any effect on religious parents' decision to send their children to state schools? Is society more harmonious when children grow up with a common educational experience?

- Is the state attentive to the wishes of all parents, or does it favour some over others? Is it reasonable that political considerations should override parental wishes?

TESTING AND TERTIARY ADMISSION

In view of education's undeniable importance for building and sustaining societies, and in view of the costs to governments for educational institutions, it is not surprising that there have long been attempts to measure and evaluate students' educational progress. This trend has been part of a larger movement to measure 'impacts' and to compare performance among organisations, systems and nations.

One important factor concerns what is being measured. Certainly, basic literacy and numeracy are fundamental skills required by any educated person. They are, however, also skills that can be acquired through rote learning, whereby competent, functional performance is achieved without too much thinking.

Is this education? Or does education demand something more — not least those higher thinking skills that underpin the human capacity for making meaning?

THE QUESTIONS

Does the focus on testing and tertiary admission levels such as ATAR (the Australian Tertiary Admission Rank) lead teachers and schools to focus on meeting or exceeding the benchmarks at the expense of true education?

In particular:

× Have we as a society properly grasped what should be the aims of education? Is education for the future being aided by testing and reporting?

× Does access to this information enable you to relate better to your child's school?

× Would you, or should you, consider changing your child's school on the basis of their ATAR (or equivalent) score?

× Is such testing having a positive influence on the focus of teachers and schools?

× Is the testing regime fair for all students? Does it lead to a fairer allocation of educational resources?

THE ELDERLY: ACTING IN THEIR INTEREST

Most people in affluent Western societies are living longer. That does not, however, necessarily mean they are living better. Whether because of disease or simply a wearing out of the body, there comes a time when the elderly are unable to care for themselves. In the past, family members would usually help, something easily done when extended families lived close to one another. Several generations were often available to help, and the elderly constituted a source of wisdom and a symbol of continuity.

Today many elderly people are placed in so-called aged-care facilities. At their best, these facilities combine comfortable and convenient living arrangements with first-rate medical care designed to meet the needs of individual residents. At their worst, the facilities are a 'holding pen' for those waiting to die. In Australia many elderly people are fortunate in being eligible for 'packages' of assistance that allow them to remain in their own home with the help they need to continue living comfortably and safely, remaining part of the wider community, in familiar surroundings and in contact with family and friends. There are, however, others who become unwell and need care in a specialist facility.

If your main concern is the welfare of your elderly loved one(s), you need to be able to distinguish between what they want and where their interests actually lie. For example, a diabetic might *want* chocolate, but a doctor will know that eating chocolate is not in the person's *interests*. It is the doctor's duty to serve interests rather than satisfy wants. In the same way, an elderly person may *want* to remain in their own home and to do so without any care or support. It might, however, be in their *interest* to be supported by additional care — either at home or within a facility that can cater for their particular needs.

While our society places high value on the personal autonomy of individuals, there can come a time when a person is unable to determine for themselves how best to proceed (perhaps because of dementia). It is in these circumstances that family members might be required to make the kind of distinctions just outlined.

THE QUESTIONS

Does the elderly person have the mental capacity to make a well-informed, autonomous decision? In doing so, are they capable of being responsible for the consequences of their own choices—or will some other person have to carry the cost in a way that might compromise their independence? Are people considering the 'least bad' option—the one that allows the elderly person to realise as many of their remaining preferences as possible—at a reasonable cost to others? Finally, can we be sure that the interests of the person with the least capacity to complain are not being sacrificed for the mere convenience of others?

In particular:

× What does the elderly person really want? Is it consistent with their interests?

× Can the family do more to support an elderly person in maintaining their preferred situation?

× What will best promote or uphold the person's dignity?

× Which of the options will best secure the person's quality of life? Will they flourish—or at least live as well and as safely as possible—in this place?

× Which option will help nourish and support not just their body but also their mind and spirit?

× Would you be willing to live in the same circumstances—if that were what was offered to you?

× Do any of the options impose an unacceptable burden or risk on another person—for example, a spouse?

⨯ Is the decision being motivated by a false sense of economy, saving money today for a promised future that an elderly loved one might never get to enjoy?

THE MARKET AND THE PROFESSIONS

Two complementary worlds intersect and affect many aspects of our lives. One is the world of the market; the other is the world of the professions.

Scottish philosopher Adam Smith saw the world of the market as one that endorses the pursuit of self-interest for the satisfaction of wants. As he argued, it need not be through a benevolent regard for others that the butcher, brewer or baker provides for our dinner: it is enough that they do so as a matter of self-interest. He reasoned that through the operation of an 'invisible hand' we will all be better off. Markets have no intrinsic value. Rather, they can be assessed to see if they are working by calculating the increase in the stock of common good they produce. If a market fails to produce an increase, it fails as the tool it is meant to be.

On the other hand, the professions are defined by their members' commitment to subordinate self-interest in serving the interests (as opposed to wants) of others. Society needs the professions to act as gate-keepers, helping keep free markets aligned with their ethical founda-tions—no lying, no cheating, no oppressive use of power—and to help prevent and, if necessary, make good the effects of market failure.

Society knows there is a potential cost to be borne by those who renounce their right to pursue self-interest, especially when all around them in the market are pursuing their own interests. Society therefore enters into a social compact whereby it offers members of the professions specific privileges, or benefits, in return for their taking on ethical commitments that place on them restrictions that are greater than those applying to market participants. Among the benefits can be respect and status, the reservation of certain types of work for them alone (closed markets) and the prospect (but not guarantee) of good remuneration.

The case of someone wanting to buy a block of chocolate offers a simple way of grasping the difference between a person operating in a market and one operating in a profession. A chocolate vendor will care little about anything other than the buyer being willing and able to pay the price being asked. As long as those two conditions are satisfied, the vendor will satisfy the customers. If, however, the purchaser is a diabetic and approaches their doctor with a request for chocolate, the doctor should refuse, regardless of the amount of money offered. This is because the doctor must act in the interest of the patient, which in this instance is not in keeping with what the chocolate enthusiast wants.

Members of the professions have specific ethical obligations that attach to the purposes they serve. Lawyers are supposed to care about the administration of justice, health professionals are supposed to care about human wellbeing, engineers are supposed to care about safety and effectiveness, accountants and journalists are supposed to care about truth.

Some people seek to enjoy the benefits of the social compact entered into by the professions without accepting the obligations. For example, a lawyer might tell you they 'just run a business in the law', that they sell their services on the same basis as a plumber, cleaner or any other service provider, operating in a marketplace, motivated by self-interest, satisfying their clients' desires. If such an approach were to become the norm, the grounds for preserving the current social compact would crumble, and the whole edifice of the professions would be seen as a sham.

THE QUESTIONS

The professions have traditionally played a vital role in society. Their capacity to do so depends on their members accepting that they have specific ethical obligations that are different from, and in some senses opposed to, those applying to people operating in the market. What happens when the professions no longer seek to honour those obligations?

In particular:

× Do the professions still have a valid role in society, or are they a relic of a different time? Could the marketplace do just as well at providing the necessary services?

× Are there some areas of life in which the pursuit of self-interest should not be allowed?

× Is the social compact between society and the professions fair for all concerned?

TIPPING, BARGAINING AND CHARITY

If you go to a shop to buy, say, a block of chocolate, in most cases the price will be fixed. All you have to do is pay the nominated amount and the chocolate is yours. Many—but not all—types of exchange have this take-it-or-leave-it nature. In some cases, though, there is a genuine opportunity to exercise discretion, especially when it comes to tipping, bargaining and making donations to charity. What then are the relevant ethical considerations in these cases?

Tipping is meant to involve a voluntary payment made in recognition of exemplary service. In some circumstances, however, it has lost its voluntary status and has become obligatory. A particular example of this is evident in the United States, where the wages paid to people working in restaurants, hotels, bars, and so on, are very low—well below the level of the Australian minimum wage. In the United States the assumption is that employees will earn the bulk of their pay through tips, the theory being that this will encourage good service as employees seek to earn the favour of their patrons. The consequence is that many people working in the US hospitality sector expect, if not demand, the payment of a gratuity, whatever the level of service. Stories of restaurant patrons being abused, even pursued down the street, because they didn't leave an adequate tip are not uncommon.

The structural arrangements for US employment have therefore warped a voluntary practice into something completely different. In Australia a growing number of hotels, bars and restaurants now impose a compulsory service charge. This is meant to ensure the payment of a gratuity, but it is hardly this if what the client thinks about the service quality is disregarded. In any event, people who are not aware of the existence of a charge often leave a tip, in addition to the amount paid through the formal charge.

The most unpleasant aspect of tipping is seen when an individual collects the tips on behalf of a group of diners, offers to pay the bill, and pockets the tips without passing them on to the staff. This might happen rarely, but it does happen, and it is either fraud or theft (take your pick): the money was provided for an acknowledged purpose and then used for another purpose without the consent of its original owners.

As for bargaining, there are some commercial environments in which everything is negotiable. This is the world of bargaining, or haggling: the price is arrived at by way of negotiation. If you don't mind a bit of uncertainty and enjoy dealing with people, bargaining can be fun and a rewarding experience. In fact, in some cultures merchants will be disappointed if a customer does not bargain, even though they receive a higher price than they otherwise would.

Bargaining is part of the performance of purchasing. It typically begins with the merchant offering to sell the object for an unrealistically high price and the purchaser offering to buy at an unrealistically low price. This is followed by a *pas de deux*, a series of graduated steps towards the destination, which is of course the sale. Along the way a number of variables other than price can be put on the table; examples are the mode and speed of payment (cash or credit) and the offer of extras such as optional additions and bulk discounts. For the customer the challenge is to work out how low the merchant will go; for the merchant the challenge is to keep the customer interested.

There are two main problems with bargaining. First, one has to be confident that the goods for sale are in fact what they purport to be: plenty of people have bargained hard only to find they have paid over the odds for a fake. The second problem warrants deeper thought: it arises when the bargain is not an equal one, when one of the parties is dominant and takes advantage of the other.

Asymmetry of this kind can occur on either side of a bargain. Someone controlling a village's only source of potable water, for example, can charge usurious rates in times of drought; the thirsty have no choice but to pay. Buyers can also use a power imbalance for their purposes; a seller of goods might be desperate, depending on a sale to feed their family, whereas the purchaser, who might not need to make the purchase at all, can drive a hard bargain. Some sellers might be so desperate they make a sale that involves a loss on their part, but having some money in their hand might be the most important thing at that time.

Harsh bargains of this kind are not really part of a free market. Since the time of Scottish philosopher Adam Smith it has been understood that a market cannot be considered free if people lie, cheat or use their power oppressively. All three things distort markets, ultimately causing them to fail. Bargaining should be free, in the sense Smith proposed. This requires both sellers and purchasers to have some idea of the fundamental value of what is being sold. Beyond covering the cost, negotiations then determine relative value.

The other example of discretionary spending considered here concerns giving to charity. Not all gifts take the form of money: many people donate goods, and a huge number work as volunteers. When it comes to money, Australian law has it that for a gift to count as a donation it must be offered without any prospect of return or reward. Those who want or need a reward are better to offer a sponsorship deal.

There are many good causes to which one can direct donations. Many charities focus on obvious areas of public concern—curing diseases, feeding the hungry, housing the homeless and so on. There is, however, a growing tendency for people to move away from funding organisations that do general good and instead look for charities with which they might have some personal connection—for example, providing funds for a Tanzanian school founded by a friend of a friend.

As it happens, the more significance you think you might derive from giving, the less altruistic your gift becomes. Some say this does not matter, that the motivation for giving is not especially relevant. What does matter, they say, is whether or not the donation is doing any good in the world, whether or not it is being applied in order to produce a demonstrable benefit. This approach has led to an increasing focus on measuring and evaluating the results of charitable endeavours. Of course, some things are easier to measure than others. It is easy to count the number of homeless people or to measure progress in curing a disease such as breast cancer; it is much harder to track the impact of, say, an ethics centre on the lives of individuals and communities. Even so, knowing that your donation does make a difference can reinforce your commitment to giving.

It is of note that philanthropic giving is now being complemented by what is referred to as 'impact investing', whereby an investor allocates funds in the expectation of making a commercial return on the condition that the circumstances of individuals or society are improved. It will be interesting to see how this blending of self-interest and social purpose affects the traditions of philanthropy.

THE QUESTIONS

Various opportunities are available for shaping the way you spend your money. Are there any general principles that apply, such that your act of discretion is ethically sound?

In particular:

- Are you being respectful to the person who might benefit from your act of discretion (such as tipping)?

- Is there an asymmetry of power or influence that you need to take into account when bargaining? If so, is it distorting the situation?

- × If there is an exchange, does it represent fair value?

- × Do you understand the context within which your decision (to make a donation, say) is being made?

- × How are you balancing a regard for others against self-interest?

- × Will your act of discretion have a beneficial impact?

- × How would you feel if you were on the receiving end of the transaction?

TRAVEL IN THIRD WORLD COUNTRIES

Many Australians choose to travel abroad. Their most popular destinations used to be in Europe and North America, but there has always been a cohort of travellers who have taken a more adventurous path. These paths can lead to and through some of the most disadvantaged places in the world. The disadvantage can be caused by famine, overpopulation, war, corruption, or a combination of these and other factors. It is possible to find yourself affluent, healthy and secure but face to face with people who have none of these advantages. What should you do?

The first thing to note is that, just as there is a difference between being hungry and starving, so there is a difference between being poor and being impoverished. Many people live perfectly contentedly with little.

A woman who lived in a thatched hut with a polished mud floor comes to mind. Her most valuable possession was a pig. There was nothing about her situation that spoke of destitution; in fact, she would have been shocked if she had thought someone might see it necessary to change her way of life. In contrast, turning a corner in India, I looked up to see a truly beautiful woman. It was only a glimpse, but I took in the fact that she was perched on a pile of rubbish, working her way through the refuse in an effort to find food and other things that would be of use. Would she have wanted to be left to her fate if there was an alternative?

The difference between my relatively affluent circumstances and the circumstances of people such as the two I describe here is largely a matter of luck. Unless you believe in some kind of karmic debt, the fact that I was born into a middle-class Australian family has nothing to do with merit on my part. Similarly, those born into poverty have done nothing to deserve their lot in life.

What then are the ethical questions that arise when travelling among the poor and oppressed? The first thing to do is to suspend your judgment until you know the facts. It would be easy to think that the woman with her pig is in the same situation as the beauty on the rubbish heap. That would be a mistake. Prudence and respect require us to set aside assumptions and instead actually find out what the individuals concerned think and feel about their circumstances.

Second, it must be remembered that compassion can be exploited by the unscrupulous. Children will be maimed at birth in order to make them successful beggars, their disfigurement being calculated to arouse compassion in the hearts of the relatively affluent. Some go on to lead lives in which they embrace their situation; all, or nearly all, of them are instruments for the enrichment of others. You need to ask yourself whether your compassionate act is actually helping the needy or simply reinforcing a cycle of cruelty and exploitation.

Third, you should ask yourself if your consumption of relative luxuries (such as multi-star hotels with air-conditioning) makes a genuine contribution to the economy, thus helping to sustain the needy. Or is it just selfish? Who profits from your consumption? How does the supply chain operate? Are local people benefiting from your presence?

Travel is about respectful interaction with other people and other cultures. This is not to say that a traveller should set aside their own ethical code and adopt that prevailing in the place they visit: to do so would be inauthentic and in its own way disrespectful. Instead, a considerate and attentive traveller will be alive to the customs and practices of the places they visit. They will be curious but not judgmental. They will aim to understand rather than condemn.

A good traveller will also aim to go from place to place treading lightly—not disturbing the places they visit but instead trying to leave each location a little better off for their having been there. How you travel is at least as important as where you go.

THE QUESTIONS

Does a traveller have special obligations when visiting the Third World? How might a traveller 'add value' to the lives of their hosts? To what extent should a traveller adapt to, or adopt, the lifestyle of the host community?

In particular:

× Are you able to look at the situation as if through the eyes of the local people? Have you spoken with them directly?

× Are you making unwarranted assumptions about the places and people you visit?

× Have you thought about your traveller's footprint?

× Is your visit making a positive contribution to the community? Do you understand the supply chain you have tapped into?

× Are there lessons to be learnt from how other people live? If so, how might these lessons be translated into the circumstances of your own life? Could other people learn from you?

× Is your interaction with the host community respectful?

× Are people trying to take advantage of your goodwill? Do you care? Would you do the same thing in similar circumstances?

UNIVERSITY FEES

The cost of attending university has varied over the years. Today, the middle ground of public opinion thinks of university education as a co-investment by the student and the state. Students obviously derive financial benefits from higher education, especially in the form of employability and lifelong income; the state derives practical benefits in the form of skill development, productivity and innovation, all of which are supported by the maintenance of core funding and fee income paid to the universities.

The current arrangements see the state fund the larger proportion of the cost of a university degree. Students are loaned the balance, although some choose to pay as they go, emerging from their course debt free. Those with a debt are required to repay the loan only after they are earning a reasonable salary, and the repayment is made over an extended period.

Since, however, an increasing number of students (including full-time students) are required to work in order to support themselves—and with employment prospects for university students starting to 'soften'—we need to ask if fee arrangements are fair. This is an especially pressing question as governments contemplate fee deregulation. Should this happen, the cost of a university education will vary from institution to institution and from course to course, but in general it is bound to increase.

THE QUESTIONS

What would be the fairest way to fund access to university degrees?

In particular:

- Should higher education be free—an investment in the future?

- Does higher education provide sufficient benefit to the nation? Would the funds be better invested in technical and further education and in skills development more generally?

- Should funding be limited to students studying degrees that are of tangible benefit to the community—for example, medicine and engineering?

- Should students fund a proportion of the cost of their studies? What is a fair proportion?

- Is it fair to people who do not go to university to use their tax dollars to fund higher education?

- What would be a fair basis for repaying loans used to fund degrees?
- Should there be an upper limit on what universities might charge for a degree?

UNPLEASANT TRUTHS

As part of my work I used to ask people what they would do if they saw the partner of one of their best friends passionately kissing another person. Some people were adamant that they should say nothing—that it was better not to become involved. Some thought they should tell their friend, as gently as possible. Most thought they would confront the unfaithful person and give them an ultimatum: own up or be exposed.

The last option has a number of advantages, the most important being that it allows for the possibility of getting the facts straight. Too often people make assumptions about what they see and get things badly wrong. I know of a case where two workmates (male and female) were regularly seen leaving work together. The man's partner knew nothing of this, but her friends told her of their suspicions—and ruined her surprise birthday party! Checking the facts is an essential first step.

There will, however, be times when the facts add up and particular assumptions are warranted. There will be times when an unpleasant, or 'inconvenient', truth will need to be told.

THE QUESTIONS

We might expect that people want to know the truth about their own circumstances and their place in the world. But what if the truth will cause hurt, to an innocent party or to a larger group? If you are convinced that the truth must be told, how do you proceed?

In particular:

- ˣ Are you sure about the facts and exactly what they mean?

- ˣ Are you relying on unwarranted assumptions?

- ˣ Are you the best person to be conveying the information?

- ˣ When is the time and where is the place most likely to be best for delivering the information—that is, to avoid causing harm or at least to minimise the harm caused?

- ˣ Is there some positive aspect of the situation that needs to form part of what is disclosed?

- ˣ Are you sure the person will want to know the truth? Or have they made it clear there are some things they would prefer not to know?

UNWANTED GIFTS

Occasionally someone gives you a gift that you genuinely do not want. The example I have in mind is when someone's grandmother knits a truly awful jumper that will only cause embarrassment if worn. She presents it with love and pride and asks the recipient to try it on. This is one of those no-win situations that can arise in life. What do you do?

Then there can be business situations when gifts and hospitality exceed what is reasonable. In business, the context is always one of 'mutual self-interest'. Knowing this, how do you respond to offers that are well in excess of normal practice or are potentially compromising? I often hear from people who have been at a business function where the hospitality has included access to sex workers. What if this is outside the bounds of your personal moral code?

Giving and receiving gifts can involve complex behaviours. Refusal of a gift can cause embarrassment and sometimes offence. The giver might be embarrassed at not having accurately gauged your preferences or ethical framework. Offence can also be caused, if your refusal to accept a gift is thought to be a repudiation of the individual or if it causes a loss of face. Yet there could be further personal dishonour if you accept a gift that compromises you or you pretend to like something you actually loathe.

THE QUESTIONS

Do you understand the cultural context of gift-giving and, in particular, the underlying values and principles that are being expressed in this context? Have you taken account of the symbolic and emotional aspects of what it means to offer, receive or refuse a gift in this context?

In particular:

- Is your moral compass well calibrated? Or do you place your personal preference (or the convenience of avoiding a 'difficult moment') ahead of ethical considerations?

- Would acceptance of the gift compromise your values and principles?

- Does your relationship with the gift giver (a relative, for example) create special obligations?

- Is the relationship strong enough to survive a candid response to the gift? For example, could you tell your grandmother you love her and you love the thought behind her gift while giving reasons why you cannot use it?

× Are there rules or guidelines that let you off the hook, enabling you to say, 'The rules that prevent me from accepting …'?

× Can the gift be accepted but not be used by you—perhaps if you register it as being available for use by others who do not risk being compromised?

VOTING

In a democracy one of the paramount privileges and obligations of citizens is to vote. Apart from any functional purpose (such as electing representatives to sit in parliament), voting is an acknowledgment that it is citizens who are the ultimate source of authority in a democracy. Other systems place authority elsewhere: in a theocracy the ultimate source of authority is god; in a plutocracy the ultimate source of authority lies with the wealthy; in an aristocracy the ultimate source of authority is in the hands of the nobility (or, originally, the virtuous). Only in a democracy do the people have the ultimate say about the system that will govern them and the identity of those who will exercise power.

For most of the history of democracy there was a restricted franchise, whereby the right to vote was limited, usually to men with property. In the late nineteenth century and early twentieth century, however—first in New Zealand and then in Australia— the right was extended to women and eventually all citizens deemed old enough to make an informed decision.

It is sometimes said that Australia has a system of compulsory voting. This is not quite correct. What Australia compels its citizens to do is collect a ballot paper. Indeed, collecting a ballot paper is one of the few things an Australian citizen *must* do. The actual voting process is secret, and nobody is obliged to cast a valid vote. As a result, if a person elects not to vote they do not have to. The downside of this is that, if a person chooses not to vote, the credibility of any complaint they might make about government policies or practices is weakened. Their complaint might be well based, but the non-voter has turned their back on the opportunity to help shape the outcome of an election and thus the policies that will be adopted by government.

One of the most basic things voters need to decide is whose interests they will take into account when casting their vote. Is it appropriate to think only of oneself or perhaps one's immediate family? Or should a voter take into account the welfare of their wider society? Further, should electors do as Irish statesman and philosopher Edmund Burke recommended and consider their duty to the past, the present and the future?[31] For example, should we be thinking of the interests of generations as yet unborn?

Finally, is there some kind of overarching idea about what would make for a good society that should guide one's vote—an idea that would allow a citizen's central values and principles to be reflected in laws, policies and social institutions?

THE QUESTIONS

Very few 'civic obligations' are imposed on Australians in return for the privileges of citizenship. Should turning up to vote be compulsory? How do we make sure our vote really counts?

---

31 Burke, E (2005), *Reflections on the Revolution in France*, http://www.gutenberg.org/files/15679/15679-h/15679-h.htm.

In particular:

× Thinking about your own values and principles, which candidate or party best aligns with your personal vision of what constitutes a good society?

× Which candidates can you most trust to keep their promises and to have the good judgment and character required to act in the best interests of your electorate and the wider community?

× Whose interests are you considering? Just your own? Those of a narrow group? Those of future generations? How might you justify the boundary you apply?

WORK COLLEAGUES' SOCIAL BEHAVIOUR

Occasionally work colleagues can find themselves in a social setting that leads to a revelation of personal characteristics that are surprising or even unnerving. Alcohol need not be involved, but it often is. For example, a person who is quiet and restrained at work might reveal themselves to be larger than life when let loose with a karaoke machine. Of course, the changes can be more startling than that, especially when social and professional inhibitions become relaxed at events such as the office Christmas party.

But you don't need to attend special workplace functions to be affected by the social habits of colleagues. Some people like to hum or sing while working, oblivious to the effect on people nearby; some like to eat pungent foods at their desk, filling the office with odours that others might find unpleasant. Others treat their piece of office space as a private preserve in which mess can run riot. And then there are those keen exercisers who return to the office fitter, hotter and happier but also a bit smellier than their colleagues might enjoy.

For the person concerned, these attributes can be perfectly natural. The garlic eaters and the joggers do not intend to disturb others or cause offence. They are being themselves. Equally, they might object to other types of behaviour—slurping rather than sipping tea, for example.

As in life generally, everyone has to compromise in a workplace. Ideally, the compromise is a matter of choice rather than necessity: it is far better if people anticipate the needs of others and voluntarily adjust their behaviour. This is not possible, however, when people are blind to the effects of their own choices: then it might be necessary to intervene—if not for your own sake, then for the sake of others.

Intervention can be tricky. The person concerned might have no idea that they are a noisy eater, for example, or that they could use some deodorant after exercising, or that their habit of humming the same tune over and over is driving other people nuts. In each of these cases the cause of others' disturbance is a personal attribute, which means that the person concerned might be embarrassed, possibly even offended, to be told that their behaviour is troubling for others. On the other hand, they might be equally embarrassed and upset if they are not told and find out some other way. So, one needs to decide if the disturbance is sufficiently serious to justify intervention. If it is, tact, good humour, sensitivity and an eye for a possible solution are essential.

There is something powerful about coming forward with a problem and then offering a potential solution. A good solution will allow the person to be themselves without having an adverse effect on others. In the examples just mentioned possible solutions could be the provision of a lunch room (with a good exhaust fan), an office shower and bathroom, headphones for staff needing quiet, and a sound baffle next to the hummer's desk.

THE QUESTIONS

How do you create and preserve a harmonious workplace in which people can be themselves without disturbing or otherwise adversely affecting their colleagues?

In particular:

× Are you aware of social boundaries in your workplace? Does your behaviour breach those boundaries by affecting your colleagues' senses?

× Is your colleague unaware of their effect on others?

× Is the source of difficulty an aspect of the individual's person or culture? Is it part of who they are?

× Have you thought about possible solutions to the problem?

× Are there tactful and sensitive measures that can be taken to let the person know there is a problem? Who would be the best person to alert them?

× What is your back-up plan if the person refuses to change their behaviour?

WORKPLACE BULLYING AND HARASSMENT

Workplace bullying and harassment not only decrease productivity; they also have the capacity to ruin the lives of individuals who are targeted. The trouble is the line between bullying and 'robust feedback' is not always clear. What defines 'harassment' is a matter for the person who is subject to the behaviour, which is as it should be.

It is reasonable to expect that employees should be open to supervision and, if required, to correction and coaching by their superiors. This sometimes involves managers having to provide feedback that is critical of an employee. Nobody likes being criticised. Equally, some managers dislike giving negative feedback to the extent that they overcompensate and become harsh and defensive as a way of coping with potential conflict. In these circumstances employees can sometimes claim they have been bullied, especially if the criticism is sustained over time and not matched with an offer of support to remedy the perceived poor performance.

Harassment can occur whenever a person behaves in a manner that another person finds inappropriate and disagreeable. This leaves wide scope for different patterns of relationship among different people, and there is thus no single, objective standard for identifying instances of harassment. Instead, a far more pragmatic and understandable approach is taken. Its essence lies in a person's right to register their discomfort and ask another to refrain from specific behaviours. Giving every person this individual right takes the guesswork out of determining how one ought to behave to others. You simply ask if the individual concerned finds the behaviour acceptable. Or you stay prepared to stop a particular behaviour the moment another person voices their objection. One possible objection to such arrangements is that they give too much power to individuals, who might be tempted to make unreasonable objections. As a safeguard, society has established a number of tribunals that can test the reasonableness of objections.

It is important to remember that not every case of bullying or harassment is deliberate. Some people are quite unaware of the effect of their presence on others and can be perceived as threatening even when that is not their intent. It would be unfair to blame people like this for anything other than a lack of self-awareness. Equally, people who find themselves affected by a particular behaviour have a responsibility to assess the nature of their own response: are they unfairly requiring another person to change simply to fit in? Either way, much misunderstanding can be avoided if people are sensitive to the effect they can have on others.

It is not easy for people to complain of bullying or harassment. They can be labelled disruptive, not a team player, unduly sensitive, unresponsive and so on. It might be necessary to draw on considerable reserves of courage to raise one's voice against bullies and those who harass.

When it is necessary to 'call someone out', ideally the complainant will not have to act alone but will be backed by a network of supporters who are ready to offer assistance. Bullies are notorious for being cowards, and their bravado can quickly vanish when they are challenged, especially if they have to face the challenge on their own.

THE QUESTIONS

How does one stand up against bullies? How does one distinguish between genuine cases of bullying and the robust exchange of opinions that can be a normal part of performance management?

In particular:

×   Are you being respectful in your treatment of other people? Are they being respectful to you?

×   Is there another agenda—for example, relating to performance— at work here? Is an allegation of bullying or harassment a proxy for some other concern?

- × Are you being overly sensitive?

- × Are you being insensitive—perhaps treating too lightly a matter that someone else considers serious?

- × Are you aware of asymmetries of power? Are people misreading the situation because of this? Are you using power or position in a way that threatens others?

- × Are you ready to change your behaviour if someone objects?

- × Is your potential objection reasonable and well founded?

- × Is there a formal mechanism whereby a report of bullying can be lodged?

- × Are there people who will stand with you should you confront a bully?

WORKPLACE ETIQUETTE

Nothing seems to raise work colleagues' hackles more than being expected to clean up a mess made by others, especially in the kitchen. It can lead to a nasty cycle of inactivity, with piles of dirty dishes and unwashed glasses growing by the day. Eventually, someone snaps and cleans everything up, perhaps hoping they will embarrass others into doing their fair share. It rarely works. Usually, old patterns of behaviour are reinforced and the cycle continues.

On one level it seems perfectly obvious that each person should be responsible for cleaning up whatever mess they make. The only exceptions would be if someone's job description actually includes this role—to clean up on behalf of everyone—or if people have agreed to take on the task, perhaps by turns. Otherwise each person is responsible for dealing with the problem directly or for making arrangements for others to do so.

In the last case, arranging for others to perform these duties might be a sensible option. For example, a skilled surgeon might be better off spending their time in the operating theatre rather than washing up after morning tea. A rational use of time and expertise might not, however, be the only, or the most important, consideration. Among other factors could be, say, respect: hospital staff might simply find it disrespectful if the surgeon assumes that the time and skills of others are less valuable.

As a rule, the time it takes to clean up after oneself is minimal, and the positive effect on the amenity of common spaces is great.

The problem is not confined to dirty dishes, though. Similar difficulties arise in relation to refrigerators (taking up more than one's fair share of space, food being left to go mouldy, and strong odours, for example), general sitting areas, shared resources, and so on. Whenever responsibility is dispersed and ill-defined there is a risk that 'freeloaders' will take advantage of the situation. Some organisations respond by making each person's obligation explicit, although it is unfortunate that this is necessary.

There are many ways of responding to colleagues who are not taking their fair share of responsibility—some ways being more mature than others. If you are bold (or nasty) enough you could place all of an individual's dirty material on their desk. Alternatively, you could speak to them directly, asking them to lift their game. Or you could simply aim for a quiet life and clean up the mess yourself. Whatever your response—and that includes doing nothing—try to avoid presenting yourself as a martyr.

THE QUESTIONS

What do we do when one or more people in the workplace are not accepting their fair share of responsibility, and common areas and amenities are being degraded?

In particular:

× Do the individuals concerned have a good reason for their behaviour?

× Are you willing to step in and fix the problem for everyone? Can you do so without becoming a martyr or being resentful?

× Are there structural solutions to the problem? For example, would the task be best allocated to a particular individual?

× When you use common facilities are you respectful of others?

× Are there reasonable measures that can be taken to make people aware of the consequences of their actions?

CONCLUDING THOUGHTS

For many people the prospect of living an 'examined life' will inspire neither interest nor joy. The idea can sound sanctimonious, an invitation to make life more difficult than it needs to be.

Some who find refuge in religious faith might consider it arrogant of humans to think we have the capacity to second-guess god's (or the gods') will. For my part, I cannot accommodate a theology that entertains the idea that a divine being would create a genuinely independent individual endowed with free will only then to have this creature turn off its brain, silence its conscience, and unthinkingly conform to the dictates of a priestly caste or the words written by men in scripture. I know this is a caricature of some theologies, which are usually far more sophisticated for those who penetrate their mysteries, but my account represents the standard experience of religion by the majority of believers.

I know, too, that every totalitarian—religious, political, cultural, whatever—will be dismayed by a philosopher's appeal to people to think about the life they choose to lead. Totalitarians are the enemy of the best in humanity. They sell us a sense of belonging by scapegoating 'the other'; they quell our opposition by labelling dissent as treason; they assuage our desire for certainty by prescribing what suits their agenda, while proscribing anything original that might emanate from a free mind.

A few people might think they are too old to take on the challenge of an examined life—too set in their ways. Why bother? Why take on another burden when it is enough to make it through each day? I understand this reluctance, especially when I have painted such a mixed picture of what it means to live such a life.

Yet, if this book demonstrates anything, it is the way in which the ethical dimension intersects with every aspect of our lives and shapes the world we make—together. Humanity's role in climate change is not a mere fact. It is a matter of choice. The same is true of how we respond to the plight of the most disadvantaged in our immediate communities and abroad. We can look the other way or we can render assistance. It is a matter of choice.

The same is true of our relationships—whether it be in connection with the very young or the very old. Along the way, we will encounter people whose lives seem to be in accordance with our personal ideals. Others will confront us with ways of living that, at first glance, seem to be strange and confronting. My counsel is to be slow to judge and aware of any unfounded prejudices that could be clouding your perceptions. This does not imply that you should abandon your values and principles or become a relativist. Instead, it is simply a matter of being genuinely open to the possibility that other ways of living might be instructive—if only to reinforce your own outlook. That, too, is a matter of choice.

For the most part our choices are reflected in the 'things' we make—not just tangible objects but also relationships, institutions and all the rest. Save for the limitations imposed by the laws of physics, these things are and become what we choose. We are therefore responsible for what we make. This is not necessarily in terms of their effect in the world, for this may be in the hands of others. Rather, we are responsible for our intentions in relation to the things we make—in particular, for whether they are fit for purposes that we reasonably believe to be good.

Every new product or organisational design, every new policy or procedure, every new system—all of it should be examined for its ethical status, with adjustments made in the design process. This approach can be applied, without great cost, in both the public and private sectors, as well as in the lives of individuals, families and communities. It is hoped that forethought will lead to more sustainable and just outcomes that serve the interests of all—including the other creatures with whom we exist.

As for the young, all is before you. You have the opportunity to fashion the world anew. This need not mean tearing up all that has gone before: the good should be honoured, the indifferent recognised, the bad learnt from. Young people offer hope. They are idealistic, with an instinct for finding meaning in life, rather than just doing a job. The only thing they might lack is sufficient confidence— confidence that it is possible to make a difference. This does not depend on grand gestures of the kind historians might record. A difference is equally made by smaller things—the ability, the willingness, to fall just on the 'right side' of every question. Bit by bit, in tiny increments, the world will change. You just need to discern the direction you want it to take.

There is nothing heroic about living an examined life. It is more difficult than a life of habit—even 'virtuous habits'. And few will stop you in the street and say, 'Well done. It's great the way you think about things.' Most people won't even notice. But it is a life fit for a human being—possibly the only life worth living for one of our kind.

I finish with a poem I wrote decades ago, when I was setting out on the adventure that has been my life thus far. Perhaps you will think of this when you come to reflect, with a calm spirit and subtle mind, on how you will respond to the questions explored in this book.

HEROISM

Some think that heroes are forged in the white heat of the dangerous moment.

But there is another kind of hero—

The person of quiet decency

Whose achievement is built only over an entire career.

We are struck by the intensity of lightning,

Yet fail to mention the thunder that rolls into the distance

Long after the lightning's moment has passed.

We are captured by the tumultuous descent of the waterfall

While forgetting the steady progress of the river.

And we marvel at the ocean's power,

Unaware that we stand on ground

Claimed for us by the silent witness of the ancient cliff.

ACKNOWLEDGEMENTS

With thanks to Rob and Jenny Ferguson, who let me be sequestered within their cottage while writing this book.

Thanks, too, to the team at Ventura Press who commissioned this work and have lavished their usual care on its publication. Special mention should be made of my editor, Chris Pirie, who has sweated over every word—for the betterment of the whole.

Finally, this book would not have been possible without the input, over a lifetime, of the many people with whom I have worked, every one of them a better teacher to me than they will have realised.